Sophia Dediu

Dim Sum
SPRING FESTIVAL

DERC Publishing House
Boston, Massachusetts, U. S. A.

Sophia Dediu   **Dim Sum**

Copyright ©2017 by Sophia Dediu

All rights reserved

Published and printed in the
United States of America

Library of Congress Cataloging in Publication Data

Sophia Dediu
Dim Sum

ISBN-13: 978-1-939757-45-6

Editor's Note

If you ever wandered what is so special about Chinese cooking, this book is the answer!

We all heard many stories about Chinese cooking, but this book comes with delicious novelties. From Peking ravioli, with a flavor of Italy, to Shanghai pastry dough, and from Wonton soup, to Dim Sum pot stickers, you almost begin to speak Chinese… There are also plenty of interesting and important information and photographs, to form a cocktail book as fancy as a couture cocktail dress for a Chinese lion's head party.

My beloved wife Sophia, who is the greatest cook under the Sun, wrote this book with love and dedication, and reading it will certainly make you feel much better!

Michael M. Dediu

Boston, USA, February 27, 2017

Sophia Dediu   Dim Sum

INTRODUCTION

Everyone likes a good story, which is as close to veracity as possible and Chinese culture has over five thousandth years full of divine civilization snd traditions which started millenia back in time.

One of the timeless folklore tales of heroes who battled demons/dragons makes the topic of the wisdom, which endured for many centuries the traditional celebration of the Dim Sum (also known as the Spring Festival), which brings forward early in the spring the virtues of ancient China.

The Dim Sum is the time when the ancient legends come to life uplifting the spirits through food and customs for old and young.

Will present three inspirational menus for three years when I attended this event: 4713-the goat, (2015); 4714-the monkey, (2016), and 4715-the rooster, (2017).

Besides cooking instructions of the traditional meals, I introduced other Chinese recipes, to expose different simple Chinese cooking techniques.

It is my hope and purpose that this book will fill some of your missing links regarding the Chinese most celebrated holiday – Dim Sum – or so called Spring Festival, celebrated in many Asian countries.

It is intended primarily for the reading public, rather than for the experts, however, I hope that the experts will find it captivating as well.

I want to thank to my husband Michael M. Dediu, for carefully reading it, offering valuable suggestions and criticism.
I want to thank to my son Horace H. Dediu for providing some of the most breath taken photos from his visits to Asia.

Everything has its beauty but not everyone sees it.

Confucius (or honorific Kŏng Fūzĭ – literally "Grand Master Kong")
September 28, 551 BC – 479 BC
Philosopher during the Spring and Autumn period in the Chinese history.

Sophia Dediu   Dim Sum

Remember every morning when you wake up:
To laugh often and loud,
To win the respect of intelligent people and affection of children,
To get the acclaim of the truthful appraisals and to endure the betrayal of hypocrites friends;
To appreciate what is beautiful and to discover what is best in everyone;
To do such that at least one soul would know what love means because you live;
To leave behind you a world a little better.

Sophia Dediu   Dim Sum

Sophia Dediu is also the author of these books (which can be found on Amazon.com):

1. Sophia Dediu: The life and its torrents – Ana. In Europe around 1920
2. Sophia Dediu: Sophia meets Japan
3. Sophia Dediu: Chocolate Cook Book: Is there such a thing as too much chocolate?

Sophia Dediu translated and managed these books (which can be found on Amazon.com):

1. Georgeta Simion – Potanga: Beyond Imagination: A Thought-provoking novel inspired from mid-20th century events
2. Ana Dediu: The poetry of my life in Europe and The USA
3. Ana Dediu: The Four Graces

Michael M. Dediu is the author of these books (which can be found on Amazon.com):

1. Aphorisms and quotations – with examples and explanations
2. Axioms, aphorisms and quotations – with examples and explanations
3. 100 Great Personalities and their Quotations
4. Professor Petre P. Teodorescu – A Great Mathematician and Engineer
5. Professor Ioan Goia – A Dedicated Engineering Professor
6. Venice (Venezia) – a new perspective. A short presentation with photographs
7. La Serenissima (Venice) - a new photographic perspective. A short presentation with many photos
8. Grand Canal – Venice. A new photographic viewpoint. A short presentation with many photos
9. Piazza San Marco – Venice. A different photographic view. A short presentation with many photos
10. Roma (Rome) - La Città Eterna. A new photographic view. A short presentation with many photos
11. Why is Rome so Fascinating? A short presentation with many photos

12. Rome, Boston and Helsinki. A short photographic presentation
13. Rome and Tokyo – two captivating cities. A short photographic presentation
14. Beautiful Places on Earth – A new photographic presentation
15. From Niagara Falls to Mount Fuji via Rome - A novel photographic presentation
16. From the USA and Canada to Italy and Japan - A fresh photographic presentation
17. Paris – Why So Many Call This City Mon Amour - A lovely photographic presentation
18. The City of Light – Paris (La Ville-Lumière) - A kaleidoscopic photographic presentation
19. Paris (Lutetia Parisiorum) – the romance capital of the world - A kaleidoscopic photographic view
20. Paris and Tokyo – a joyful photographic presentation. With a preamble about the Universe
21. From USA to Japan via Canada – A cheerful photographic documentary
22. 200 Wonderful Places, In The Last 50 Years – A personal photographic documentary
23. Must see places in USA and Japan - A kaleidoscopic photographic documentary
24. Grandeurs of the World - A kaleidoscopic photographic documentary
25. Corneliu Leu – writer on the same wavelength as Mark Twain. An American viewpoint
26. From Berkeley to Pompeii via Rome – A kaleidoscopic photographic documentary
27. From America to Europe via Japan - A kaleidoscopic photographic documentary
28. Discover America and Japan - A photographic documentary
29. J. R. Lucas – philosopher on a creative parallel with Plato, An American viewpoint
30. From America to Switzerland via France - A photographic documentary
31. From Bretton Woods to New York via Cape Cod - A photographic documentary

Sophia Dediu  Dim Sum

32. Splendid Places on the Atlantic Coast of the U. S. A. - A photographic documentary
33. Fourteen nice Cities on three Continents - A photographic documentary
34. 17 Picturesque Cities on the World Map - A photographic documentary
35. Unforgettable Places from Four Continents, including Trump buildings - A photographic documentary
36. Dediu Newsletter, Volume 1, Number 1, 6 December 2016 – Monthly news, review, comments and suggestions for a better and wiser world
37. Dediu Newsletter, Volume 1, Number 2, 6 January 2017 (available at www.derc.com).
38. Dediu Newsletter, Volume 1, Number 3, 6 February 2017 (available at www.derc.com).

Sophia Dediu — Dim Sum

ABOUT THE SPRING FESTIVAL AND TRADITIONAL DIM SUM
Provided by my Chinese friends and colleagues

Chinese New Year known also as the Spring Festival celebration originated from an ancient Chinese tradition of a monster/dragon called Nian. It is said that Nian was a creature half lion half unicorn which dwells in the mountains. Once a year at new year's eve it comes out of its nest to attack neighboring villages. But the villagers had learned that after living years and years in a cave has made Nian sensitive to loud noise and bright colors, particularly the color red, and that's where the tradition of fireworks, firecrackers, drums and red ornaments comes from.

Words are the voice of the heart. - Confucius

Sophia Dediu　　　　　Dim Sum

Nian is the Chinese word for year.
Customs in China are very different from those in the West. Understanding such customs is the key to successfully enjoy travelling there or getting together with Chinese friends and colleagues. The New Year celebration or Spring Festival lasts 15 days and takes place between mid-January and beginning of February following the Lunar Calendar.

Traditionally, the biggest event of any Chinese New Year's eve is the dinner (Nian Yen Fan), which is a dish consisting of special meats served at the tables of Chinese families, as a main course for the dinner.

This meal is comparable to Thanksgiving dinner in the U.S. and similar to Christmas dinner in other countries with a high percentage of Christians.
Food photos are a celebration of shape and color and though it's true for food anywhere, it's especially true for the Chinese cuisine. Luckily, you can find dishes from all around China without setting a foot in China.

In the first day of the Spring Festival families get together for a reunion to see each other, to find out how they survived the winter and to wish each other the best for the New Year to come.

Sophia Dediu　　　Dim Sum

After dinner, some families (older generations) go to local temples hours before the New Year begins to pray for a prosperous new year.
As in many other cultures they will light the first incense of the year.

The younger generations will hold parties and even hold a countdown to the New Year.

This tradition started during Han dynasty and continued to take place at different dates based on the Lunar calendar. In 1911 China adopted the Gregorian calendar celebrating the New Year at January 1. During the Cultural Revolution in China it has been decided the return to the Lunar calendar to celebrate the New Year.

In the Lunar calendar the New Year is celebrated at the end of the first month of the Lunar calendar which is in mid-January and beginning of February. The Lunar calendar is structured on the Moon phases.

Sophia Dediu   Dim Sum

The Spring Festival is the most celebrated and the longest Chinese holiday.
It is the time to enjoy being alive and reflect on the ancient traditions and culture Each year gets assigned an animal according to the Chinese zodiac which is a cycle of 12 years.

The legend is that when Buddha was Lord, he called all animals to join him on the New Year celebration. Only 12 showed up. He named each year after these animals: Rat, Ox, Tiger, Rabbit, Dragon, Snake, Horse Goat, Monkey, Rooster, Dog, and Pig.

Sophia Dediu   Dim Sum

During the Spring Festival, people shop for new cloth, shoes and special ingredients for the festive sumptuous meal, and fire crackers.
People dress in red, which is the color of happiness. On the front doors are hanged spring couplets written in black on a red paper.

There are numerous customs like displays of decorations of bright red and golden paper. The red and golden are considered as bringing luck and prosperity. The tables are dressed with red tablecloth and golden napkins.

The centerpieces, in general, small Chinese characters are inspiring health, wealth, good luck, happiness and longevity. To please the Zao Jun (the kitchen God) the host offers a ceremonial sacrifice. In front of his poster they offer the Nian Gao, which are sticky rice cakes. The tradition says that by pleasing Zao Jun, their house hold will be protected.

Sophia Dediu   Dim Sum

The houses are decorated with fresh plants and flowers. In the Chinese culture the evergreen plants symbolize longevity. The flowers used during this occasion are arrangements of blooming plants like prunes, bamboo, pine. Pomegranates which symbolize fertility and the pine tree eternal youth.

Traditional foods are Jiaozi – steamed Chinese dumplings; these are done mainly in the North part of the country. They will hide a coin in one of the dumplings; this is good luck for the founder. Dumplings symbolize wealth because their shape resembles a Chinese sycee. I

In the South part of the country it is customary to make a glutinous New Year cake Nian Gao – sticky rice pudding and send pieces of it as gifts to relatives and friends in the coming days of the new year. Niángāo literally means "new year cake" with a meaning of "increasingly prosperous year in year out".

Many dishes served have a special symbolism. The fish is cooked and served as a whole piece symbolizing abundance, the chicken symbolizes good luck. Both, the fish and the chicken are served with head and tail symbolizing abundance and good luck from beginning to the end of the year.

The tray of togetherness – chuen-hop – which is octagonal or oval form with eight compartments filled with symbolic foods such as dates, nuts, winter melon, lychee, lotus seeds, carrot, coconut, lotus root water chestnut, tangerines

Sophia Dediu   Dim Sum

After the meal elders pass out red envelops - Hong Bao abundance and good luck. On the outside is written New Year and inside are placed money.

Traditionally, bamboo stalks, and recently, firecrackers are lit to scare away evil spirits. The house's doors are shut locked, not to be reopened until the new morning in a special ritual of opening the door of fortune.

During the two weeks of celebration people are resting.
During the New Year people observe some traditional customs.

Sweeping the house on the first day of Chinese New Year should be avoided as it is symbolic of sweeping away good luck. In general they avoid cutting their hair on the first day of New Year as hair symbolizes prosperity and cutting or washing them could cut or wash their prosperity away Crying or quarrelling should be eliminated as it is believed that it will set a precedent for the New Year.

The 15 day is the lantern festival which concludes the holiday.
During the lantern festival, children go out at night to temples carrying paper lanterns.
This tradition has been traced back 200 BC. During the Han dynasty the Emperor put lanterns around his house to pay tribute to the Universe. The paper lanterns are decorated with painted zodiac signs, animals, flowers, birds, ritual symbols.

Sophia Dediu   **Dim Sum**

The new year paper cuttings and couplets is the pasting of big diamond shapes adorned in calligraphy is the inverted Chinese character (fú /foo/) over doors. These foo (meaning good fortune) characters are purposely inverted as they want Good Fortune to shower on those coming in through the door. This tradition is believed to have derived from an innocent mistake when a family attached their 'foo upside down as a mistake.

In some regions the Chinese dragon dance became the main show. The dragon long of about ten feet is made of silk, bamboo and paper. The dragon is steered in the air by men and the dance is accompanied by marching bands.

Sophia Dediu — Dim Sum

Every year, in our country, the Chinese restaurants hold an open house party at the start of Chinese New which features help-make-it-and-then-eat-it dim sum foods (and an 8 treasure pudding, which is really a banquet item but great fun and guaranteed to impress people - it looks very spectacular, and can't fail to turn it out if you follow the directions).

Here in the U.S. the Dim Sum is a Chinese sort of brunch, or tea. If you go into a Dim Sum restaurant in a Chinese area, you will find a huge variety of steamed dumplings, soups, noodles, and pastries, served with your choice of teas. Delicious! And usually, anywhere I've been, a great bargain considering the variety and quantity of food available, even ignoring the amount of skill it takes to properly fold the various dumplings and pastries.

The flowers in the Chinese culture have a distinguished significance

The showy flowering plant Peony of genus Paeonialarge, with its globe-shaped, red, white, pink, Native to: Europe, Asia, North America is esteemed as one of the most exquisite flowers.
The peony is a symbol for nobility and value. The peony became popular in the imperial palaces during the Sui and Tang dynasties reason for which it is considered the king of flowers.

It is a spring flower and, therefore a symbol of spring. In China it is used also as a representation for female beauty and reproduction.

Sophia Dediu   Dim Sum

Orchid:
The orchids (family: Orchidaceae) is the symbol of perfection and abundance. It is emblematical of fertility, and encourages for plenty of children.

Sophia Dediu   Dim Sum

The narcissus plant with its yellow and white flower with a cup shaped center, in China is a symbol which is said to give the flowering of our concealed talents. It is supposed to supplement the hard work; reassuring those who will do so will be rewarded in their lives.

Sophia Dediu   Dim Sum

The meaning of Lotus.
Buddhists all over the world recognize this Lotus as signifying the holy seat of the Buddha. To the Chinese it symbolizes ultimate purity and perfection because it rises untainted and beautifully from the mud.

The Chinese use this plant in its entirety roots and petals.
It is used for its medicinal properties.
According to the Buddhist philosophy the whole plant has a profound significance conveying the true nature of reality.

Sophia Dediu   Dim Sum

Hydrangea with its white, pink, or blue flowers, in large clusters and a variety of shapes is the symbol of love, gratitude, and enlightenment. It is said that the observer can easily get lost in its abundance of beautiful petals, and thus gets lost in one's own thoughts – propitiating higher thought and reaching enlightenment.

Due to its versatility and beauty the Chinese people use the hydrangea for a thank you gift to an anonymous hero in their lives.

Sophia Dediu  Dim Sum

Chrysanthemum signifies a life of ease.
Chinese and Japanese Buddhist are using these flowers as offerings on alters in temples.

The Chrysanthemum is the Imperial seal of Japan

It is also the symbol of powerful Yang energy; therefore it will appeal to good luck in the home.

Sophia Dediu   Dim Sum

Dim Sum isn't normally served after early afternoon or so (except when they make it at home). If you go into a dim sum restaurant after 2 PM or so, you'll often find the whole kitchen staff seated around tables, folding the dumplings for the next day's lunch. It's pretty amazing to watch, especially if you have tried to make the same foods at home and had they come out sloppy-looking. It's on par with watching your grandmother make her own strudel dough.

Gung Hay Hsin Nien
Happy New Year!

DIM SUM FOOD MENUS

Sophia Dediu — Dim Sum

DIM SUM PARTY YEAR 4713

Began February 19, 2015
The Goat Year, the 8th position on the Chinese Zodiac
People born on the Goat year are creative, intelligent and dependable.

Gung Hay Hsin Nien
Happy New Year!

Sophia Dediu  Dim Sum

Menu

Flaky Moon Cakes
Pot Stickers (Peking Ravioli)
Si Shi Sha Bing (Fluffy Shrimp Cakes)
Congyou Bing (Oily Scallion Cakes)
Ba Bao Fan (Eight Precious Rice Pudding)
Cantonese Turnip Cake
Sheng Ren Bing (Almond Cookies)
Lop Cheung Bow (Sausage Buns)
Cha Siu Bow (Barbecued Pork Buns)
Chinese Bun Dough
Shu Mai (Pork Dumplings)
Glutinous Rice Balls
Fried Wonton
Stuffed Bananas
Pork-Stuffed Mushrooms
Chun Guen (Spring Rolls)
Lo Bo Si Bing (Flaky Turnip Cakes)
Jia Yao Guo (Crunchy Cashews)
Tianzha netao (Sweet Fried Nuts)
Shanghai Pastry Dough
Gah Li Gai So Bang (Curried Chicken Pastry)
Dai Gut Yau Gok (Good Luck Dumplings)
Stuffed Bitter Melon with Fermented Black Beans
Winter Melon Soup

Who revenge should dig two graves. - Quote Chinese

Sophia Dediu   **Dim Sum**

Sophia Dediu — Dim Sum

Flaky Moon Cakes
Ingredients

Filling
2 cups red bean paste
Skin
2 cups flour
4 tbsp. lard
8 tbsp. water
1/2 tbsp. sugar
(1/3 tsp salt)
Dough
1 cup flour
4 tbsp. lard

Process

Filling: Divide filling into 20 balls.
Skin: Mix and knead, then divide into 20 pieces.
Dough: Mix and knead, then divide into 20 pieces.

1. Roll each piece of skin into a circle, put a piece of dough in the middle, and wrap up to enclose the dough.
2. Roll each one out into a 2x4 inch rectangle. Roll up starting at the short end.
3. Roll each one out into a 1x4 inch rectangle.
4. Roll up starting at a short end into a one-inch square.
5. Roll into a 2 inch circle. Put a piece of filling in the center and seal skin around it. Flatten into a 2 inch circle.
6. Bake at 350° F for 20 minutes.
Makes 20 cakes.

Sophia Dediu — Dim Sum

Pot Stickers (Peking Ravioli)
Ingredients

Skin
2 1/2 cup flour
2/3 cup boiling water
2/3 cup cold water
1/2 cup flour (during kneading)

Filling
2/3 lb. ground pork
1/4 lb. chopped Chinese chives (or scallions)
1 cup chopped bamboo shoots
 (1 tsp salt)
3 tbsp. sesame oil
1/4 tsp black pepper

Process

Make the filling
Mix everything together and divide into 36 portions.

Make the Skin
1. Add boiling water and then cold water to flour. Knead and let rest ten minutes.
2. Divide into 36 pieces and roll into 2x4 inch ovals.

Making dumplings:
1. Put a piece of filling in each skin, fold in half, and pinch to seal.
2. Heat pan and 4T oil. Line pan with dumplings, flat side down.
3. Fry one minute on low heat until brown.
4. Add 1/2 c hot water and cover. Cook until water evaporates.
5. Invert on plate to serve.

Dipping sauce:
Soy sauce
Sesame oil
Worcestershire sauce
Chopped garlic
Makes 3 dozen.

Sophia Dediu — Dim Sum

Si Shi Sha Bing (Fluffy Shrimp Cakes)

Ingredients

Cakes
1 lb. shrimp, shelled, deveined, and minced
2-3 oz. water chestnuts, chopped
3 eggs
2 tsps rice wine or sherry
(1 tsp salt)
3 ginger slices
2 scallions
2 tbsp. cornstarch
3 tbsp. vegetable oil for frying
Sauce:
3 tbsp. sugar
3 tbsp. vinegar
7 ginger slices, peeled and shredded

Process

1. Mix shrimp, water chestnuts, eggs, sherry, (salt,) ginger, scallions, and cornstarch. Form into balls.
2. Mix sauce.
3. Heat oil and fry balls until brown.
4. Serve with dipping sauce.

Sophia Dediu Dim Sum

Congyou Bing (Oily Scallion Cakes)
Ingredients

3 cup flour
1 cup water
10-15 scallions, chopped
1 1/2 tsp sesame oil
(2 tsp salt)
3 tbsp. peanut oil

Process

1. Mix flour and water to a very stiff dough. Let rest for thirty minutes.
2. Divide dough into six pieces. Roll each into a very large circle.
3. Sprinkle salt on each, then oil.
4. Sprinkle scallions on each.
5. Roll up tightly, pinching ends to keep scallions inside.
6. Coil up rolls. Just before cooking, roll each coil out into an 8 inch circle.
7. Fry in oil until golden brown. Cut into wedges to serve.

Makes six cakes.

Sophia Dediu — Dim Sum

Ba Bao Fan (Eight Precious Rice Pudding)

Ingredients

Pudding
1 1/2 cup glutinous rice
5 tbsp. sugar
Butter to grease bowl
1/4 cup mixed candied fruits
1/4 cup raisins
1/4 cup pitted dates
1/4 cup candied lotus seeds or walnuts
1 cup sweet bean filling

Sauce:
1/4 cup sugar
1 tbsp. cornstarch
1 1/4 cup water
1 tsp almond extract

Process

1. Wash rice and drain. Cook with 2 1/4 c water, simmering until soft (fifteen minutes).
2. Mix in sugar and turn off heat.
3. Grease a seven-inch bowl. Put half of the candied fruit in the center. Then arrange raisins, dates, lotus seeds, and the rest of the candied fruit into an eight-petal flower.
4. Cover with half of the rice. Put bean filling in the center and cover evenly with the rest of the rice.

Cooking:
1. Steam for thirty minutes.
2. Invert on a platter.
3. Boil sauce ingredients until thick and pour over pudding.
Makes one pudding.

Sophia Dediu   Dim Sum

Cantonese Turnip Cake
Ingredients

2 1/2 lb. Chinese turnips
1 cup water
2 cup long-grain rice flour
5 tbsp. oil
1 tbsp. finely chopped scallions
4 black mushrooms, soaked, stemmed, boiled twenty minutes, and chopped
1/2 cup dried shrimp, chopped, soaked in 1 T rice wine or sherry
4 Chinese sausages, chopped
(2 tsp salt)
1/2 tsp sugar
1/2 tsp pepper
1 tbsp. fresh cilantro (coriander), chopped
1 tbsp. toasted sesame seeds

Process
1. Peel and grate turnips. Simmer in water one hour or until tender.
2. Mix rice flour and drained turnips in bowl until mixture is the consistency of thick oatmeal. Add 2 T oil, mix well, and set aside.
3. Heat 2 T oil in wok. Stir-fry scallions, mushrooms, shrimps, and sausages and add to turnip mixture.
4. Add (salt,) sugar, and pepper. Mix thoroughly.
5. Grease a loaf pan and pour in mixture. Sprinkle with cilantro and sesame seeds. Place on rack in steamer and steam one hour.
6. Cool and refrigerate overnight.
7. To serve, slice and fry until golden brown.
Serves 4-6.

Sophia Dediu   Dim Sum

Sheng Ren Bing (Almond Cookies)
Ingredients

1/4 cup lard
1 cup sugar
2 tbsp. vegetable oil
1/4 tsp sesame oil
1 egg
1 cup sweet rice flour
1 tsp baking powder
(1/2 tsp salt)
1 tsp almond extract
1/3 cup chopped almonds
Whole almonds for garnish

Process

1. Cream lard and sugar. Add oils and egg.
2. Sift together flour, baking powder (and salt). Add to sugar mixture and mix well.
3. Add chopped almonds and almond extract. Mix well.
4. Form dough into one inch balls. Top each with an almond.

Cooking:
1. Place balls 2 inches apart on greased cookie sheets.
2. Bake twenty minutes at 350° F.

Makes two dozen.

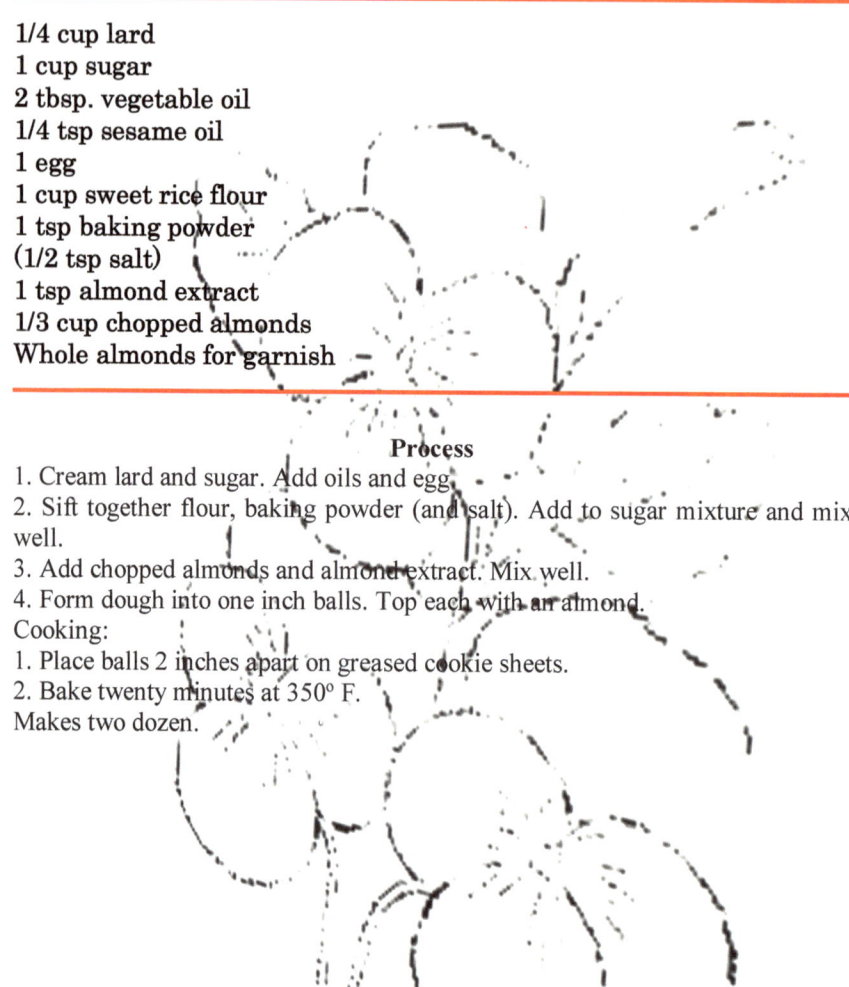

Sophia Dediu   Dim Sum

Lop Cheung Bow (Sausage Buns)
Ingredients

Dough

1/2 recipe bun dough
Filling
6 pairs of Chinese sausages, cut in halves (24 pieces)

Wrapping

1. Divide dough in 24 balls. Roll each into a two-inch circle.
2. Roll up a sausage piece in each, leaving the ends open.
3. Place seam side down on a square of wax paper.
4. Let rise one hour.

Cooking:

Steam for ten minutes, or bake at 350° F for 20-25 minutes after brushing with egg whites, water, and sugar.
Makes two dozen.

Sophia Dediu — Dim Sum

Cha Siu Bow (Barbecued Pork Buns)

Ingredients

Dough: one recipe of bun dough
Filling
4 cup finely diced Chinese barbecued pork
1/2 cup chopped onions
Sauce
2 tsp hoisin sauce
2 tsp rice wine or sherry
4 tsp oyster sauce
2 tsp catsup
1 tsp sugar
1 1/2 tbsp. cornstarch
1 1/2 cup chicken broth

Process

1. Mix sauce in small saucepan. Cook over high heat until it thickens.
2. Stir in pork and onions.
3. Chill 3-4 hours.

Wrapping:
1. Divide filling in 24 portions and dough into 24 balls.
2. Roll out each ball, leaving center thicker than edges, into a 4 inch circle.
3. Put filling portion in center of dough, gather up sides around filling, and twist to seal. Put on 2 inch square of wax paper, twist side down.
4. Put buns on cookie sheet and let rise one hour.

Cooking:
1. Steam for fifteen minutes, or bake at 350° F for 20-25 minutes after brushing with egg white, 1 t water, and 1/4 t sugar.

Makes two dozen.

Sophia Dediu — Dim Sum

Chinese Bun Dough

Ingredients

For two dozen large buns:
1 oz. yeast
1 3/4 cup warm water (110 degrees)
3/4 cup sugar
1 tsp baking powder
6 1/2 cup un-sifted all-purpose flour

Process

1. Dissolve yeast and sugar in warm water.
2. Add baking powder, then flour.
3. Knead dough for 20 minutes, until elastic and smooth (a great job for a food processor).
4. Put in greased bowl, cover with damp cloth, and let rise until it doubles in bulk.
5. Punch down and knead for five minutes.
6. Fill buns and cook.

Sophia Dediu — Dim Sum

Shu Mai (Pork Dumplings)
Ingredients

1 lb. wonton skins -- round off corners
Filling
1 lb. lean ground pork
1 cup black mushrooms, soaked and diced
1 cup fresh shrimp, cleaned, deveined, and cut in small pieces
1 small can water chestnuts, chopped fine
3 scallions, minced
1 cup Chinese cabbage, chopped
Seasonings
3 tbsp. light soy sauce
(1 tsp salt)
1/2 tsp garlic powder
1 tsp sesame oil
Dipping sauce
2 tbsp. dark soy sauce
1 tsp white vinegar
1 tsp sesame oil
1 tbsp. chopped ginger

Process

1. Combine all ingredients and seasonings and mix well.
2. Fill each skin with about 1 T of filling and fold like a tulip bulb.
3. Seal the excess skin with water and gather skin together.
4. In a wok, add about 1 cup of water. Cover and bring water to a boil.
5. Put shu mais into bamboo steamers on top of wax paper splashed with sesame oil.
6. Remove cover and add shu mai trays. Steam fifteen minutes with cover on.

Sophia Dediu — Dim Sum

Glutinous Rice Balls

Ingredients

Filling
1 cup red bean paste
Skin:
2 cup glutinous rice powder
5 tbsp. sugar
2/3 cup water
1 cup white sesame seeds
6 cup oil for frying

Process

1. Divide red bean paste into 16 portions.
2. Mix skin ingredients into smooth dough. Slightly oil work surface. Put dough on work surface and knead until smooth. Roll into a long roll and cut into 16 pieces.
3. Flatten each piece of dough into a 2-inch circle. Place a portion of filling in the middle and gather edges of skin together to enclose the filling. Roll each filled skin into a ball. Dip in water and coat outside with sesame seeds.
4. Heat oil for deep-frying. Deep-fry balls over medium heat for five minutes until expanded and golden.
Remove, drain, and serve.

Sophia Dediu   Dim Sum

Fried Wonton
Ingredients

1 lb. wonton skins
1/2 lb. ground pork
1/2 tbsp. corn starch
1 tbsp. soy sauce
1 tsp rice wine
1 tbsp. oil
(1/2 tsp salt)
2 tbsp. minced soaked black mushrooms
2 tbsp. minced bamboo shoots
1 tsp minced scallions

Process

1. Mix ground pork with corn starch, soy sauce, and wine.
2. Put 1 Tbsp. oil in skillet and cook pork 2 minutes. Add remaining filling ingredients and put in a large bowl. Mix well and set to cool.
3. Fold wontons.
4. Deep fry in hot oil (375 degrees F) until golden brown.
5. Serve with duck sauce.

Sophia Dediu   Dim Sum

Stuffed Bananas
Ingredients

1/6 lb. shelled shrimp
1/2 oz. pork fat
Marinade
(1/3 tsp salt)
1/2 tsp sesame oil
1 tsp rice wine
1/8 tsp black pepper
1/2 tbsp. corn starch
2 medium-sized, not-too-ripe, bananas
2 tbsp. corn starch
Batter
1/2 cup flour
6 tbsp. water
(1/4 tsp salt)
1/2 tsp baking powder
1 tbsp. peanut oil
6 cup oil for frying

Process
1. Chop shrimp and pork fat finely and mix with marinade.
2. Peel bananas and cut each into three sections. Cut each section into four slices lengthwise. Coat the cut surfaces of each banana section with cornstarch.
3. Spread filling on 12 sections and top each section with the corresponding plain section to make twelve sandwiches.
4. Mix up batter.
5. Coat each banana section with batter.
6. Heat oil for deep-frying. Drop banana sandwiches into oil and deep-fry for three minutes over medium heat until golden.
Remove and drain.

Sophia Dediu — Dim Sum

Pork-Stuffed Mushrooms
Ingredients

8-10 2-inch diameter fresh mushrooms
1/2 lb. lean pork, cut into small chunks
1/4 lb. raw shrimp (shelled and deveined)
4 water chestnuts, finely chopped
2 tbsp. cornstarch
(1/2 tsp salt)
1 tsp sugar
2 tbsp. soy sauce
8-10 spring of cilantro (Chinese parsley) - optional

Process
1. Wash and dry mushrooms. Remove stems.
2. Chop shrimp and pork in food processor. Mix with water chestnuts, cornstarch, (salt,) sugar, and soy sauce.
3. Stuff mushrooms.
4. Place mushrooms on a heatproof serving dish with a rim. Put cilantro over mushrooms. Cover dish with a double thickness of waxed paper.
5. Steam for 40 minutes.

Sophia Dediu   Dim Sum

Chun Guen (Spring Rolls)
Ingredients

1 package spring roll skins
2 cup cooked ham
5 black mushrooms
1 cup bamboo shoots
1 cup shredded Napa cabbage
1/2 lb. fresh bean sprouts
3 stalks celery
2 stalks scallions
Sauce
(1 tsp salt)
2 tsp sugar
2 tbsp. oyster sauce
2 t cornstarch
1/4 cup chicken broth
4 cup oil, for deep-frying
1 egg, beaten

Process

1. Soak mushrooms until soft. Discard stems.
2. Slice ham, mushrooms, bamboo shoots, and onions to the size of a match stick. Slice celery on the diagonal into strips of the same size. Rinse bean sprouts in cold water and drain well.
3. Mix sauce.
4. Heat wok, add 1T oil, and separately stir-fry and set aside: the bean sprouts (one minute), the celery (two minutes), the Napa cabbage (2 minutes), and the ham (2 minutes), adding more oil as needed. Pour sauce mixture over ham and mix until sauce thickens (will get very thick). Mix in the other ingredients and let cool.
5. Position each skin like a diamond. Put 1/3c filling on lower section of skin. Roll firmly about half-way up the skin. Moisten remaining three corners with egg. Fold side corners in and roll up completely.
6. Deep fry spring rolls and both sides until golden brown, turning once. Drain and serve.

Sophia Dediu   Dim Sum

Lo Bo Si Bing (Flaky Turnip Cakes)
Ingredients

2 1/2 cup finely shredded daikon
(1 tsp salt)
1 1/2 cup peanut oil
1/2 lb. Chinese sausages cut into 1/4-inch dice
Filling seasoning
2 tsp rice wine
(1/2 tsp salt)
1/4 tsp black pepper
2 tsp sesame oil
2 cup all-purpose flour
1 cup cake flour
(1 t salt)
2/3 cup lard (or butter)
1/3 cup ice water

Process
1. Put shredded turnip in bowl with salt. Let sit 20 minutes. Squeeze out accumulated water.
2. Heat 1/2 T oil in wok and stir-fry sausages for two minutes, until golden and most of fat has rendered.
3. Remove all but 2T oil and stir-fry turnip until tender, about two minutes. Add sausage and filling seasonings. Cook 30 seconds.
Refrigerate until cold.
4. Combine flours (and salt). Cut in shortening until mixture looks like cornmeal. Add water and mix until smooth. Wrap dough in plastic wrap and refrigerate 20 minutes.
5. Roll out dough into a rectangle about 1/6 inch thick. Cut 4-inch circles. Gather scraps up and chill 15 minutes. Roll out again and cut more circles (should produce a total of 24).
6. Place a tbsp. of filling in center of dough circle. Gather up edges and pinch to seal. Flatten into around about 2 1/2 inches in diameter.
7. Heat skillet and add remaining oil. Heat to 375 degrees F. Fry cakes on both sides until crisp and golden brown, about five minutes per side.

Sophia Dediu — Dim Sum

Jia Yao Guo (Crunchy Cashews)
Ingredients

2 cup water
4 tbsp. honey
(1 tsp salt)
1/2 lb. raw cashews
6 cup peanut oil

Process

1. Place water, honey (and salt) in saucepan and stir to dissolve the honey. Add cashews and heat until boiling. Reduce heat to medium and cook uncovered for fifteen minutes. Remove cashews, drain, and air-dry for an hour, turning occasionally.
2. Heat oil in wok to 350° F. Add cashews and deep-fry until golden brown. Remove nuts and drain on brown paper. Cool completely before serving.

Sophia Dediu   Dim Sum

Tianzha netao (Sweet Fried Nuts)
Ingredients

2 cup shelled pecan halves
3-4 cup boiling water
1/2 cup sugar
1 tbsp. water
3 cup peanut oil

Process
1. Cover nuts with boiling water and soak for three minutes.
2. Drain nuts and mix with sugar. Add 1 t water if necessary to make sugar stick to nuts.
3. Put sugared nuts on a dry plate and dry overnight or longer.
4. Heat oil in wok. Fry nuts until they are golden brown and sugar coating is crisp and candy like. Dry on a plate and break apart to serve.

Sophia Dediu   Dim Sum

Shanghai Pastry Dough
Ingredients

Mixture 1
1 1/2 cup flour
4 oz. + 1 tbsp. hot water
Mixture 2
1 1/2 cup flour
8 1/2 tbsp. lard

Process

1. Mix first mixture. Knead until elastic, sprinkling with flour as needed. Set aside under a damp cloth.
2. Work second mixture together. Knead until smooth. Wrap in plastic wrap until ready to use.
3. Divide each mixture into 3 equal pieces.
4. Working with one-third of each dough at a time, roll mixture 1 into a rectangle. Put second mixture into center and fold first over it.

Roll out again and fold in thirds. Repeat. Set aside and do the same with the other 2/3 of the dough mixtures.

Sophia Dediu — Dim Sum

Gah Li Gai So Bang (Curried Chicken Pastry)

Ingredients

3/4 lb. boneless chicken breasts cut into 1/4-inch dice
Marinade
(1 1/2 tsp salt)
2 1/2 tsp sugar
1 1/2 tsp sesame oil
1 1/2 tbsp. oyster sauce
1 tbsp. cornstarch
1/8 tsp white pepper
3/4 tsp light soy sauce
6 water chestnuts cut into 1/8 inch dice
6 tbsp. celery, cut into 1/8 inch dice
3 tsp coriander, finely chopped
3 scallions, finely chopped
2 tbsp. curry powder mixed with 2 Tbsp. cold water
3 tbsp. peanut oil
2 cloves garlic
1 1/2 tbsp. rice wine
1-2 tbsp. chicken broth, if needed
Shanghai pastry dough
4-5 c peanut oil

Process

1. Marinate chicken in marinade for one hour. Set aside.
2. Mix water chestnuts, celery, coriander, scallions. Set aside.
3. Mix curry powder and water and set aside.
4. Heat oil in wok. Fry garlic, and then add curry powder mixture. Stir-fry 1 to 1 1/2 minutes.
5. Add chicken and marinade. Cook 30 seconds in thin layer. Mix into curry.
6. Add wine around edges of wok. Mix. Add vegetables and stir together. If too thick, add chicken broth.
7. Refrigerate overnight.
8. Roll each pastry dough piece into a ten-inch square and roll up. Cut each roll into 10 pieces. Flatten pieces and roll into 3 1/4 inch circles.
9. Place 1 T curried chicken in center of dough circle. Fold into half-moon shape and squeeze rim to seal. Make decorative scalloped edge with side of thumb.
10. Deep-fry 6 at a time at 300 degrees F until brown.

Sophia Dediu   **Dim Sum**

Sophia Dediu — Dim Sum

Dai Gut Yau Gok (Good Luck Dumplings)

Ingredients

---

2 cup flour
¼ cup sugar
5 tbsp. lard or peanut oil
3 ½ oz. cold water
½ cup peanuts with skins
¼ cup sesame seeds
3 ½ tbsp. dark brown sugar
4 cup peanut oil

Process

1. Mix sugar and flour. Work in oil. Work in water. Knead ten minutes. Set aside, covered with damp cloth, for two hours.
2. Roast peanuts in wok for 2 minutes in single layer. Turn over and roast until deep brown. Remove peanuts and peel skins. Put half of the peanuts on a sheet of wax paper and crush with a rolling pin until coarsely broken. Crush remaining peanuts.
3. Roast sesame seeds the same way, but don't crush.
4. Combine peanuts, sesame seeds, and brown sugar.
5. Cut dough in thirds. Work on one section at a time; keep the rest under a damp cloth. Roll 1/3 of dough into 12-inch rope. Cut into 12 pieces.
6. Roll each piece into a ball and roll out into 3 1/2 - inch circle.
7. Put filling on each piece, close into half-moon shape, and crimp edge to form scalloped edge.
8. Deep-fry until golden brown.

Sophia Dediu   Dim Sum

Stuffed Bitter Melon with Fermented Black Beans

Ingredients

2/3 lb. bitter melons
1/2 lb. ground pork
(1/3 tsp salt)
1 tsp minced garlic
Dash sesame oil
1/2 tbsp. cornstarch
1 hot red pepper
1 tbsp. fermented black beans
(1/3 tsp salt)
1/2 tsp sugar
1 cup water

Process

1. Discard ends of melons and slice melons 1/3" thick. Remove seeds.
2. Bring a half pot of water to a boil (add 1/2 t salt) and boil melon slices for 2 minutes. Remove and plunge into cold water.
3. Shred the hot pepper.
4. Mix ground pork, (salt,) garlic, sesame oil, and cornstarch to make filling.
5. Sprinkle cornstarch in melons, then stuff.
6. Heat 3 Tbsp. oil in wok. Fry melons on both sides until golden brown. Remove. Reheat wok with 2 T oil. Stir-fry black beans and hot pepper until fragrant.
7. Add melon, (salt,) sugar, and water. Cover and cook over medium heat for 8 minutes, or until liquid is reduced to 1/3 cup.

Sophia Dediu   Dim Sum

Sophia Dediu **Dim Sum**

Winter Melon Soup
Ingredients

Large can chicken broth
1 chicken breast
1 winter melon or large piece
6 black mushrooms
1/2 cup dried lotus seeds, optional
1 piece dried tangerine peel (1 1/2")
1 ounce Virginia ham
2 slices fresh ginger
1/2 cup sliced water chestnuts
1/2 cup sliced bamboo shoot, optional
1 tbsp. rice wine
1 tbsp. sugar
(Salt)
Pepper

Process

1. Remove strings and seeds from melon.
2. Soak mushrooms, lotus seeds, and tangerine peel in hot water.
3. Poach chicken breast in broth until cooked (10 minutes). Remove.
4. Dice ham and put in broth.
5. Dice melon flesh and put in broth. (You can do a dramatic presentation of this soup by steaming it inside a whole winter melon in a covered pan of hot water for 3-4 hours. Soup can be served from the melon.)
6. Add ginger. Drain and slice mushrooms. Add mushrooms, water chestnuts, tangerine peel, and bamboo shoots. Season with rice wine, sugar, (salt and pepper.
7. Cook until melon is tender. Remove tangerine peel and ginger slices.
8. Dice cooked chicken and add.

Sophia Dediu — Dim Sum

DIM SOM PARTY YEAR 4714

Began February 8, 2016.
The Monkey Year, the 9th position on the Chinese zodiac.
People born in the Monkey year are curious and clever.

Gung Hay Hsin Nien
Happy New Year!

To study and not think it is a waste. To think and not study is dangerous

Confucius September 28, 551 BC – 479 BC

Sophia Dediu — Dim Sum

Menu

Flaky Moon Cakes
Pot Stickers (Peking Ravioli) (Gau Ji)
Si Shi Sha Bing (Fluffy Shrimp Cakes)
Congyou Bing (Oily Scallion Cakes)
Ba Bao Fan (Eight Precious Rice Pudding)
Cantonese Turnip Cake (Dzin Lor Bok Goh)
Sheng Ren Bing (Almond Cookies)
Lop Cheung Bow (Sausage Buns)
Cha Siu Bow (Barbecued Pork Buns)
Lo Bo Si Bing (Flaky Turnip Cakes)
Tianzha netao (Sweet Fried Nuts)
Dai Gut Yau Gok (Good Luck Dumplings)
Aromatic Spiced Beef
Almond Float (Xing Ren Dou Fu)
Stuffed Potato Cakes (See Jai Bang)
Hot and Sour Soup (Suen Lot Tong)
Wonton Soup
Sweet Sesame Bows (Ch'iao Gwo)
Water Dumplings (Soi Gau)
Glazed Walnuts
Moon Cakes (Yue Bing)

Sophia Dediu   Dim Sum

Tianzha netao (Sweet Fried Nuts)
Ingredients

2 cup shelled pecan halves
3-4 cups boiling water
1/2 c sugar
1 tbsp. water
3 cups peanut oil

Process
1. Cover nuts with boiling water and soak for three minutes.
2. Drain nuts and mix with sugar. Add 1 t water if necessary to make sugar stick to nuts.
3. Put sugared nuts on a dry plate and dry overnight or longer.
4. Heat oil in wok. Fry nuts until they are golden brown and sugar coating is crisp and candy like. Dry on a plate and break apart to serve.

Sophia Dediu — Dim Sum

Aromatic Spiced Beef

Ingredients

---

2 shins of beef
10 cups water
5 tbsp. sugar
5 tbsp. soy sauce
2 tbsp. salt
6 star anise
3 tbsp. sherry

Process

1. Trim meat of external fat and membranes.
2. Boil water in large pot; add anise and beef. Boil briskly, uncovered, for 90 minutes.
3. Add sugar, soy sauce, and salt. Simmer covered for 2 1/2 hours.
4. Add the sherry. Cook uncovered until liquid is reduced to 1-2 cups.
   Strain the liquid in flat-bottom container and refrigerate to gel. Remove hardened fat from top.
5. Chill meat. Slice and arrange on tray.
6. Cut gelatin into small cubes and garnish meat with it. Garnish with coriander if desired.

Sophia Dediu — Dim Sum

Almond Float (Xing Ren Dou Fu)

Ingredients

1 envelope unflavored gelatin
1/3 cup sugar
1 cup milk
2 tsp almond extract
Green or pink food coloring (if desired)
1/3 cup cold water
3/4 cup boiling water
1 can lychee fruits
1 can loquat fruits
1 jar maraschino cherries (if desired)
1 small can pineapple chunks

Process

1. Soften gelatin in 1/3 cup of cold water in a mixing bowl.
2. Add 3/4 c boiling water and stir until completely dissolved.
3. Add sugar and mix well.
4. Add milk and mix well.
5. Add almond extract and mix well.
6. Add food coloring if desired to shade.
7. Chill in refrigerator 8-10 hours or overnight.
8. Cut gelatin into cubes and serve fruit over gelatin with syrup from the lychees.

Sophia Dediu   Dim Sum

Stuffed Potato Cakes (See Jai Bang)
Ingredients

Potato pastry:
2 cup cooked and mashed potatoes (about 1 - 1 1/4 lb.) (1 tsp salt)
½ tsp sugar
1/8 tsp white pepper
1/4 tsp five-spice powder
Mash potatoes with the rest of the seasonings.

Filing:
1/2 cup minced ham
1/3 cup minced water chestnuts
3 tbsp. minced scallions
2 t oil
(1/4 tsp salt)
1 tsp sugar
1/8 tsp white pepper
1/4 tsp five-spice powder
1/2 tsp sherry
1/2 tsp light soy sauce
Cilantro (Chinese parsley)

Process

1. Heat 2 t oil in wok, and stir-fry ham, water chestnuts, and scallions for 1 minute.
2. Add the rest of the filling ingredients.
3. Mix well and cool in refrigerator for at least 2 hours.
4. To wrap cakes: take about 1 T potato pastry, roll into a ball, and flatten in your palm to a 2-inch round. Put 1 t filling in the middle, close, and <u>flatten</u>. Press a leaf of cilantro on each side for decoration.
5. Brown in a little oil on both sides. Serve with mixture of light soy sauce, sesame oil, and vinegar.
    Makes 24 cakes.

Sophia Dediu   Dim Sum

Hot and Sour Soup (Suen Lot Tong)
Ingredients

½ lb. lean pork or roast pork, shredded thin
1 small can bamboo shoots, shredded thin
1 oz. (3/4 c) golden needles
½ cup (1/2 oz.) wood ears
1 oz. Chinese black mushrooms, soaked in hot water one hour
2 large bean curds cut in cubes
1 large can chicken broth (College Inn)
1 beaten egg
Seasonings:
(1tsp salt)
1-2 tbsp. dark soy sauce
1 tsp sugar
(1/4 tsp MSG)
2 tbsp. white vinegar, to taste
1 t black pepper, to taste
2 tsp sesame oil, to taste
1 tsp chili oil, to taste
2 tbsp. cornstarch, mixed with 1/4 c cold water, for thickening

Process
1. Soak the golden needles, wood ears, and mushrooms in hot water.
2. Shred the pork and bamboo shoots.
3. Cut the bean curd into small cubes.
4. Beat the egg and set aside.

Cooking:
1. Combine chicken broth and all ingredients except egg in large pot.
2. Add (salt,) dark soy sauce, sugar, (MSG,) and cornstarch mixture.
3. Turn heat off and add egg, slowly, in circular motion above pot.
4. Stir well.
5. Add vinegar and black pepper.
6. Remove from heat and add sesame oil to taste.
7. Add chili oil and mix well.

Sophia Dediu — Dim Sum

Wonton Soup

Ingredients

Wontons (half recipe)
1 large can chicken broth (College Inn)
1/2 can cold water
2-3 cup bok choy, sliced diagonally thin
1 oz. black mushrooms, soaked and sliced thin
1 tbsp. minced scallions (for garnish)
1/2 lb. roast pork, sliced thin
1/2-1 tsp sesame oil

Process

1. Boil wontons in water 4-5 minutes or until they float. Remove and drain under cold running water for two minutes.

2. Boil chicken broth, water, and mushrooms for 10 minutes.
3. Simmer 10 to 20 minutes.
4. Add bok choy and bring to a quick boil.
5. Add wontons, roast pork, scallions, and sesame oil, and serve.

Sophia Dediu — Dim Sum

Sweet Sesame Bows (Ch'iao Gwo)

Ingredients

2 cup flour
6 tbsp. sugar
3 1/2 tbsp. lard or butter
1/2 tsp vanilla extract (optional)
1 egg
About 1/4 cup cold water
2 tbsp. white sesame seeds
About 3 cups oil for deep-frying

Process

1. Rub together flour, sugar, fat, and vanilla. Add egg. Knead to mix well. Add water, a little at a time, until dough is soft but not sticky.
2. Put sesame seeds on a plate. Roll dough in the sesame seeds until it is generously coated.
3. Turn dough onto a floured surface. Roll into a 1/8" thin long sheet.
    Cut into 3" x 1" strips. Make a 1" split lengthwise in the middle of each strip. Pull one end of each strip through the hole, forming a bow.
4. Heat oil to 375 degrees F. Deep-fry bows, several at a time, until golden brown. Drain and cool on paper towels. Store in covered container.

Sophia Dediu — Dim Sum

Water Dumplings (Soi Gau)

Ingredients

1 lb. ground pork
1/4 lb. diced shrimp
1/3 cup bamboo shoots, diced
1/3 cup water chestnuts, diced
1/3 cup scallions, finely chopped
2 tbsp. pork fat, diced
1-2 tbsp. cilantro, finely chopped
(2 1/4 tsp salt)
3 1/4 tsp sugar
1 1/2 tsp sesame oil
Pinch white pepper
2 tbsp. tapioca flour
1 egg, beaten
1 lb. shu mai skins

Process

1. Mix well all ingredients except shu mai skins and egg and refrigerate 4 hours.
2. Place 1 1/2 - 2 tsps of filling in center of each skin. Brush egg around edges and fold skin into half-moon shape, and press together.
3. Cook in boiling water 5 to 7 minutes. Drain and serve.

Sophia Dediu — Dim Sum

Glazed Walnuts
Ingredients

1 ½ cup sugar
½ cup corn syrup
½ cup water
(1/4 tsp salt)
1 tbsp. oil
2 cups walnut meats

Process
1. Cook sugar, syrup, (salt,) and water to 300 degrees F on a candy thermometer (hard-crack stage).
2. Remove from heat and stir in oil.
3. Dip walnut pieces into syrup with slotted spoon or sieve.
4. Drain and turn out on wax paper.
5. Separate with chopsticks or a fork and let dry.
6. Store tightly covered.

Sophia Dediu — Dim Sum

Moon Cakes (Yue Bing)
Ingredients

Crust:
4 cups flour
1 tbsp. baking powder
¾ cup dried milk powder
(1 tsp salt)
3 eggs
1 ¼ cups sugar
¾ cup shortening or butter, melted and cooled to room temperature
1 ½ tsp vanilla extract

Filling:
1 cup chopped pitted dates
½ cup sweetened flaked coconut
1 cup coarsely chopped walnuts or pecans
1 cup apricot preserves
½ cup raisins

Glaze:
1 lightly beaten egg
2 tbsp. water

Process

1. Sift together flour, baking powder, (salt,) and dried milk powder.
    Break eggs into a bowl, add sugar, and beat vigorously until a ribbon is formed (five minutes). Add melted shortening, vanilla extract, and sifted dry ingredients to egg mixture, folding after each addition. Mix to a rough dough. Turn out onto a lightly floured surface. Knead to a smooth dough. Form the dough into a long roll and cut into 24 pieces.
2. Mix the filling and divide into 24 portions.
3. Using fingers press each dough piece into a 3-inch circle, with the edges thin and the center thick. Place a portion of filling in the center, gather up the edges to enclose the filling, and pinch to seal. Roll the cake into a ball and press it seam side up into a moon cake press.
4. Lightly grease baking sheet. Invert moon cakes onto baking sheet 1 inch apart. Brush moon cakes with glaze.
5. Bake at 375° F for 30 minutes, until golden brown. Cool and serve.

DIM SUM PARTY YEAR 4715

Year 4715 begins January 28, 2017.
The Rooster Year in the 10th position on the Chinese zodiac.
People born in this year are assertive, devoted, and straightforward

Gung Hay Hsin Nien
Happy New Year!

Sophia Dediu **Dim Sum**

Menu

Lotus Root Chips
Cold Noodles in Sesame Sauce
Water Dumplings (Soi Gau)
Aromatic Spiced Beef
Sweet Fried Nuts (Tianzha Netao)
Chinese Bun Dough
Sausage Buns (Lop Cheung Bow)
Barbecued Pork Buns (Cha Siu Bow)
Almond Cookies (Sheng Ren Bing)
Cantonese Turnip Cake (Dzin Lor Bok Goh)
Eight Precious Rice Pudding (Ba Bao Fan)
Oily Scallion Cakes (Congyou Bing)
Pot Stickers (Peking Ravioli) (Gau Ji)
Flaky Moon Cakes
Hot and Sour Soup (Suen Lot Tong)
Glutinous Shao Mai (Luo Mi Shao Mai)
Ginger Chicken Wontons
Coconut Tarts
Cantonese Moon Cakes (Yue Bing)
Curry Meat Turnovers
Tea Eggs
Steamed Meat Dumplings (Shao Mai)
Butterfly Cookies (Jow Wu Deep)
Sesame Cookies (Gee Ma Bang)

Who asks is a fool for five minutes, but he who does not ask remains stupid forever. - Chinese Proverb

Lotus Root Chips
Ingredients

2 lotus root sections
2 cups peanut oil
Salt to taste

Process
1. Peel lotus root with vegetable peeler.
2. Cut crosswise into 1/16-inch slices.
3. Deep-fry at 370 of until golden brown.
4. Remove, drain well, and sprinkle with salt.

Sophia Dediu   **Dim Sum**

Cold Noodles in Sesa

Me Sauce

Ingredients

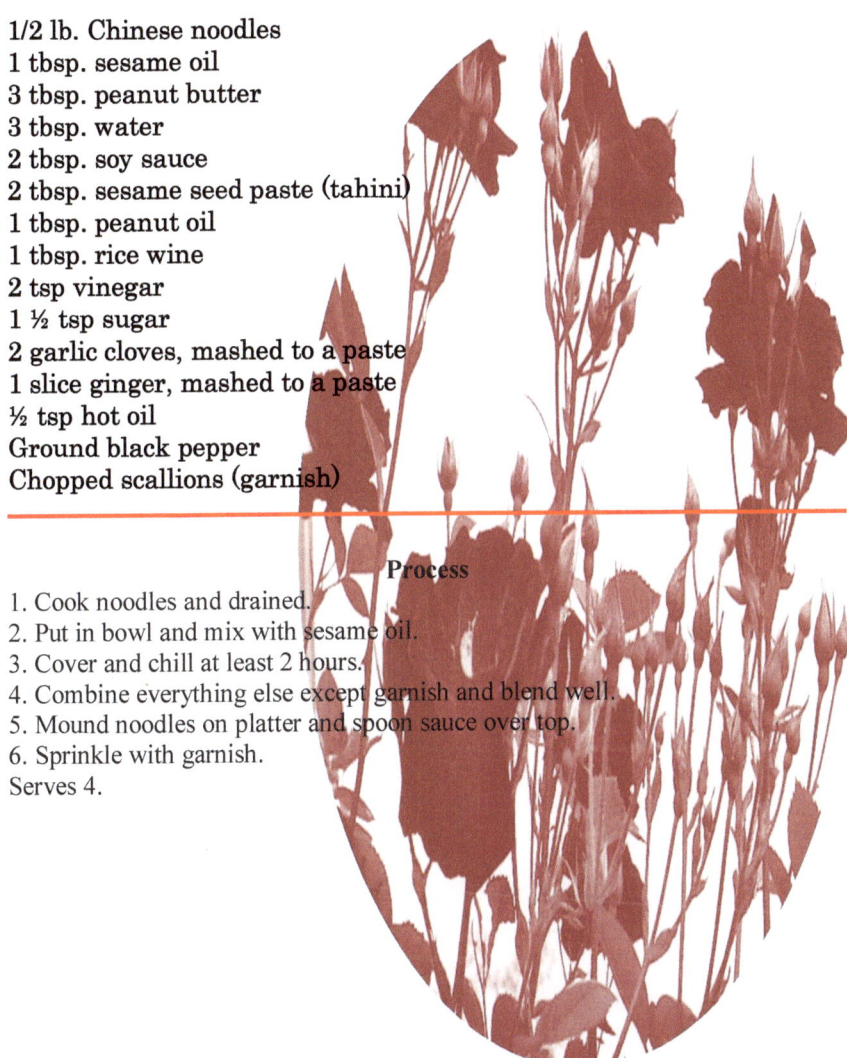

1/2 lb. Chinese noodles
1 tbsp. sesame oil
3 tbsp. peanut butter
3 tbsp. water
2 tbsp. soy sauce
2 tbsp. sesame seed paste (tahini)
1 tbsp. peanut oil
1 tbsp. rice wine
2 tsp vinegar
1 ½ tsp sugar
2 garlic cloves, mashed to a paste
1 slice ginger, mashed to a paste
½ tsp hot oil
Ground black pepper
Chopped scallions (garnish)

Process

1. Cook noodles and drained.
2. Put in bowl and mix with sesame oil.
3. Cover and chill at least 2 hours.
4. Combine everything else except garnish and blend well.
5. Mound noodles on platter and spoon sauce over top.
6. Sprinkle with garnish.
Serves 4.

Sophia Dediu   Dim Sum

Sweet Fried Nuts (Tianzha Netao)
Ingredients

2 cups shelled pecan halves
3-4 cup boiling water
1/2 cup sugar
1 tsp water
3 cups peanut oil

Process
1. Cover nuts with boiling water and soak for three minutes.
2. Drain nuts and mix with sugar. Add 1 t water if necessary to make sugar stick to nuts.
3. Put sugared nuts on a dry plate and dry overnight or longer.
4. Heat oil in wok. Fry nuts until they are golden brown and sugar coating is crisp and candy like. Dry on a plate and break apart to serve.

Sausage Buns (Lop Cheung Bow)
Ingredients

Dough:
1/2 recipe Chinese bun dough
Filling:
6 pairs of Chinese sausages, cut in halves (24 pieces)

Process

Wrapping:
1. Divide dough in 24 balls. Roll each into a two-inch circle.
2. Roll up a sausage piece in each, leaving the ends open.
3. Place seam side down on a square of wax paper.
4. Let rise one hour.
Cooking:
Steam for ten minutes, or bake at 350° F for 20-25 minutes after brushing with egg whites, water, and sugar.
Makes two dozen.

Sophia Dediu — Dim Sum

Barbecued Pork Buns (Cha Siu Bow)
Ingredients

Dough:
One recipe of Chinese bun dough
Filling:
4 cups finely diced Chinese barbecued pork (2 lb.)
½ cup chopped onions
Sauce:
2 tsp hoisin sauce
2 tsp rice wine or sherry
4 tsp oyster sauce
2 tsp catsup
1 tsp sugar
1 1/2 tbsp. cornstarch
1 ½ cups chicken broth

Process
1. Mix sauce in small saucepan. Cook over high heat until it thickens.
2. Stir in pork and onions.
3. Chill 3-4 hours.

Wrapping:
1. Divide filling in 24 portions and dough into 24 balls.
2. Roll out each ball, leaving center thicker than edges, into a 4 inch circle.
3. Put filling portion in center of dough, gather up sides around filling, and twist to seal. Put on 2 inch square of wax paper, twist side down.
4. Put buns on cookie sheet and let rise one hour.

Cooking:
1. Steam for fifteen minutes, or bake at 350° F for 20-25 minutes after brushing with egg white, 1 t water, and 1/4 t sugar.
Makes two dozen.

Almond Cookies (Sheng Ren Bing)
Ingredients

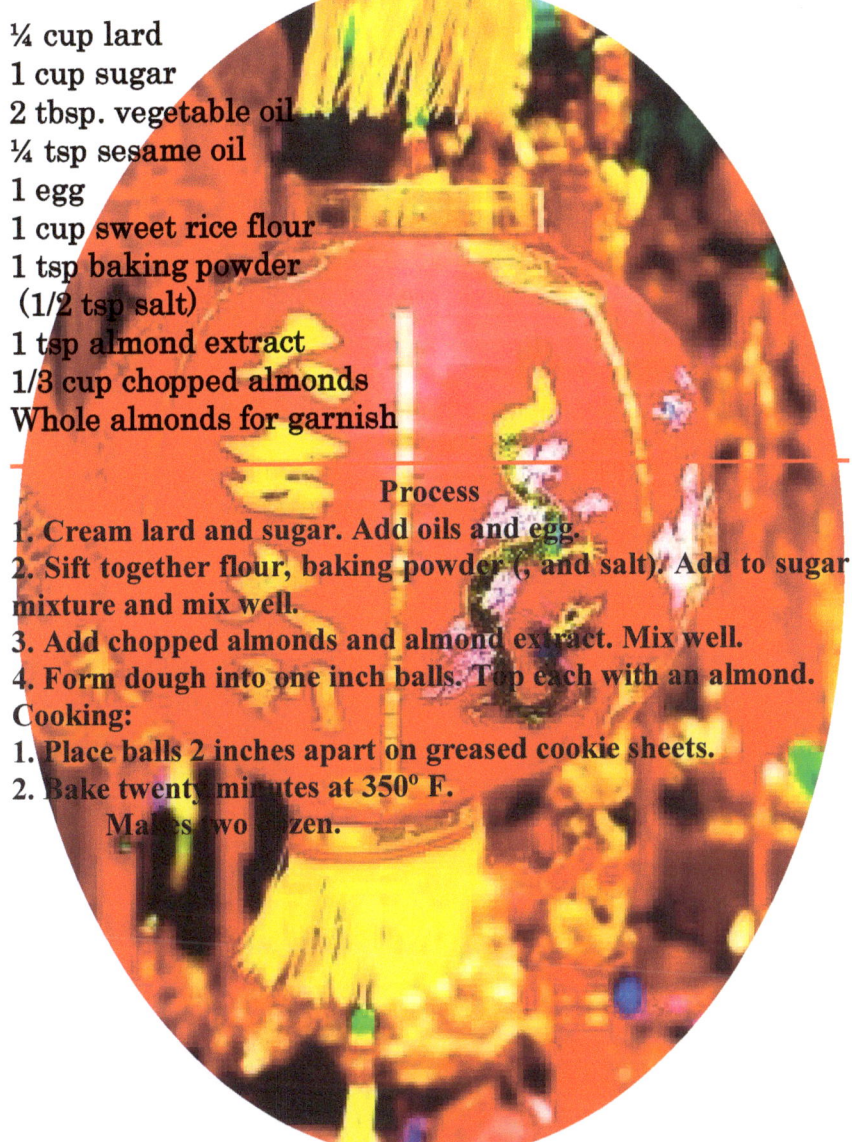

¼ cup lard
1 cup sugar
2 tbsp. vegetable oil
¼ tsp sesame oil
1 egg
1 cup sweet rice flour
1 tsp baking powder
 (1/2 tsp salt)
1 tsp almond extract
1/3 cup chopped almonds
Whole almonds for garnish

Process
1. Cream lard and sugar. Add oils and egg.
2. Sift together flour, baking powder (, and salt). Add to sugar mixture and mix well.
3. Add chopped almonds and almond extract. Mix well.
4. Form dough into one inch balls. Top each with an almond.
Cooking:
1. Place balls 2 inches apart on greased cookie sheets.
2. Bake twenty minutes at 350º F.
    Makes two dozen.

Sophia Dediu — Dim Sum

Cantonese Turnip Cake (Dzin Lor Bok Goh)
Ingredients

2 1/2 lb. Chinese turnips
1 cup water
2 cups long-grain rice flour
5 tbsp. oil
1 tbsp. finely chopped scallions
4 black mushrooms, soaked, stemmed, boiled twenty minutes, and chopped
½ cup dried shrimp, chopped, soaked in 1 T rice wine or sherry
4 Chinese sausages, chopped
2 tsp salt)
½ tsp sugar
½ tsp pepper
1 tbsp. fresh cilantro (coriander), chopped
1 tbsp. toasted sesame seeds

Process
1. Peel and grate turnips. Simmer in water one hour or until tender.
2. Mix rice flour and drained turnips in bowl until mixture is the consistency of thick oatmeal. Add 2 T oil, mix well, and set aside.
3. Heat 2 T oil in wok. Stir-fry scallions, mushrooms, shrimps, and sausages and add to turnip mixture.
4. Add (salt,) sugar, and pepper. Mix thoroughly.
5. Grease a loaf pan and pour in mixture. Sprinkle with cilantro and sesame seeds. Place on rack in steamer and steam one hour.
6. Cool and refrigerate overnight.
7. To serve, slice and fry until golden brown.
   Serves 4-6.

Sophia Dediu — Dim Sum

Oily Scallion Cakes (Congyou Bing)
Ingredients

3 cup flour
1 cup water
10-15 scallions, chopped
1 ½ tsp sesame oil
 (2 tsp salt)
3 tbsp. peanut oil

Process

1. Mix flour and water to a very stiff dough. Let rest for thirty minutes.
2. Divide dough into six pieces. Roll each into a very large circle.
3. Sprinkle salt on each, then oil.
4. Sprinkle scallions on each.
5. Roll up tightly, pinching ends to keep scallions inside.
6. Coil up rolls. Just before cooking, roll each coil out into an 8 inch circle.
7. Fry in oil until golden brown. Cut into wedges to serve.

Makes six cakes.

Sophia Dediu — Dim Sum

Glutinous Shao Mai (Luo Mi Shao Mai)
Ingredients

Filling:
1 cup glutinous (sweet) rice
2 tbsp. peanut oil
Garnishes:
½ cup dried black mushrooms, soaked and diced
1 ½ cup diced cooked pork loin
½ cup diced cooked shrimp
¼ cup minced scallion greens
Sauce:
3 tbsp. soy sauce
2 tbsp. rice wine
1 tsp sesame oil
1 tsp sugar
¼ tsp black pepper
2 tbsp. chicken broth
1 lb. shao mai skins

Process

Rinse rice. Soak in cold water one hour. Drain and cook in 1 c water.
When water boils, lower heat, cover, and simmer 20 minutes. Turn off heat and let stand ten minutes. Uncover and cool to room temperature.
Heat oil in wok and stir-fry mushrooms 15 seconds. Add other garnishes and mix.
Add rice and mix.
Add sauce and mix.
Divide filling into 36 portions.
Line steamers with moist cheesecloth or muslin or with wax paper with holes punched in it. Place filling portion on center of skin. Gather up edges, squeeze to make a "waist", flatten bottom, and smooth top with a wet spoon. Place in trays 1/4 inch apart.
Steam 15 minutes over high heat.
Serve with soy sauce.
Makes 36 dumplings.

Sophia Dediu — Dim Sum

Ginger Chicken Wontons
Ingredients

2 dried black mushrooms
1 clove garlic
2 slices ginger, peeled
Small can water chestnuts, drained
½ lb. boned chicken, cut into 1-inch pieces
2 tsp soy sauce
1 tsp cornstarch
1 tsp rice wine
½ tsp dried red pepper flakes
60 wonton wrappers (1 lb.)
Oil for deep-frying

Process

Soak mushrooms in warm water until soft. Drain and discard stems.
Drop garlic and ginger into running food processor and chop finely. Add mushrooms, water chestnuts, and chicken, and chop finely.
Add soy sauce, cornstarch, wine, pepper flakes, and blend for five seconds.
Fill wontons.
Deep fry at 350° F until golden, or cook in soup.

Sophia Dediu — Dim Sum

Coconut Tarts
Ingredients

Filling:
4 cup coconut
½ cup butter
2 egg yolks
9 oz. evaporate milk

Dough:
1 ¼ cup flour
3 tbsp. milk powder
¼ tsp baking powder
1 tbsp. Vanilla extract
½ cup butter
¼ cup sugar
1 egg

Glaze:
2 egg yolks
1 tbsp. melted butter
20 tart molds

Process

Mix filling and divide into 20 portions.

Sift flour, milk powder, and baking powder together. Add vanilla, butter, sugar, and egg and knead until smooth. Divide into 20 portions.

Preheat oven to 350º F. Press dough portion into mold. Put filling in mold.

Bake 25 minutes.

Brush immediately with egg yolks and melted butter.
Makes 20.

Sophia Dediu — Dim Sum

Cantonese Moon Cakes (Yue Bing)
Ingredients

Filling:
20 salty-egg yolks (omit if not available)
4 cup red bean paste
1 egg yolk
1 moon cake mold
¾ cup melted butter
Dough:
4 ½ cup flour
½ cup powdered milk
½ tbsp. baking powder
1 ¼ cup sugar
4 eggs

Process

Preheat oven to 350º F.

Place egg yolks on cookie sheet and bake ten minutes. Remove.

Divide bean paste into 20 portions. Roll bean paste into ball around egg yolk. Sift together flour through baking powder.

Beat sugar and eggs. Add melted butter, then flour, and mix well. Divide into 20 portions.

Preheat oven to 400 F. Flatten dough piece into 4-inch circle. Put filling in and wrap up, pinching edges together. Roll into a smooth ball. Flour mold and press ball into mold. Tap to remove.

Place on cookie sheet and brush with egg yolk.

Bake 30 minutes.

Use lotus nut paste, date paste, or white bean paste instead of red bean paste. Omit salty egg yolks if not available.

Makes 20.

Sophia Dediu　　　Dim Sum

Curry Meat Turnovers
Ingredients

Filling:
1 lb. ground pork
1 ½ cup minced onions
3 tbsp. curry powder
1 ½ tbsp. sugar
(1 tsp salt)
¾ cup water
1 ½ tbsp. cornstarch mixed with 1 1/2 T water

Skin:
2 cup flour
5 tbsp. pork fat
10 tbsp. water
(1/4 tsp salt)

Dough:
1 cup flour
5 tbsp. pork fat
1 beaten egg yolk

Process

Heat wok and add 4 tbsp. oil. Stir fry onion until fragrant. Add curry powder. Add ground pork and stir fry until cooked. Add sugar through water and bring to a boil. Add cornstarch mixture to thicken. Let cool.

Mix skin ingredients. Knead until smooth, let stand 20 minutes, and cut into 20 pieces.

Mix dough ingredients and cut into 20 pieces.

Prepare dough and skin as for flaky moon cake dough.

Roll pieces into 3" circles. Place 1 1/2 tbsp. filling in center. Fold dough in half and pinch to seal. Fold edge over and pleat. Brush one side with egg yolk.

Preheat oven to 375 F. Bake, egg side up, for 20 minutes.

Tea Eggs
Ingredients

1 piece dried tangerine peel, soaked
4 eggs
3 tbsp. black or lychee tea
1 whole star anise
¼ cup soy sauce
1 cinnamon stick
Plum sauce for dipping

Process
1. Cover eggs with cold water.
2. Bring to a boil and simmer fifteen minutes.
3. Remove eggs and cool under running water.
4. Tap each egg all over with the back of a spoon to crack the shell.
5. Bring water to a boil again; add tea, star anise, tangerine peel, soy sauce, and cinnamon.
6. Add eggs and simmer for an hour, turning often.
7. Remove from heat and let stand for an hour.
8. Remove eggs. Cool and shell.
9. Serve cut in halves or quarters, with plum sauce.

Sophia Dediu   Dim Sum

Sophia Dediu   Dim Sum

Steamed Meat Dumplings (Shao Mai)
Ingredients

---

1 lb. shao mai skins
11 oz. ground pork
1 tbsp. sugar
1 tbsp. rice wine
1 tbsp. sesame oil
3 ½ oz. onion, minced
1 oz. dried shrimp, soaked and chopped
2 tbsp. green peas

Process
1. Mix meat, seasonings, onions, and shrimp.
2. Fill shao mai skins, leaving tops open with peas showing.
3. Steam 10-13 minutes.

Sophia Dediu — Dim Sum

Butterfly cookies (jow wu deep)

Ingredients

1 lb. wonton skins
1 cup powdered sugar
Oil for deep frying

Process
1. Cut each wonton wrapper into 2 rectangles.
2. Lay one rectangle on top of the other, and make three 1/2" slits in the center, lengthwise.
3. Form a bow by pulling one end of the double pieces through the middle slit.
4. Deep fry until golden, one minute or less.
5. Drain on paper towels.
6. Sift powdered sugar over both sides.
7. Cool.
Makes 80. These keep well in an air-tight container.

Sophia Dediu   Dim Sum

Sesame cookies (gee ma bang)
Ingredients

½ cup granulated sugar
½ cup brown sugar
1 egg
½ lb. lard (no substitute)
½ tsp almond extract
2 cups flour
½ tsp baking soda
¾ tsp baking powder
Sesame seeds

Process
1. Sift flour with baking soda and baking powder.
2. Cream egg and lard.
3. Add sugars and almond extract.
4. Gradually add dry ingredients and mix well.
5. Roll 1t dough in hands to form ball, then coat with sesame seeds.
6. Place balls 3/4" apart on cookie sheets.
7. Bake in pre-heated 350° F oven 8-10 minutes.
 Makes 10 dozen. These keep well in air-tight containers.

Sophia Dediu Dim Sum

OTHER RECEPIES

When first setting foot in China or Japan it's usually the food that worries people the most. Because it's hard to trust your instincts at the beginning. Everything is so different in appearance, smell and taste. Many people are brave enough to venture into this uncharted territory of flavor.

Therefore we have compiled a list of other common Chinese dishes you can't go wrong with.

SPICY FROITE SALADE

When is hot outside you don't feel serving soup with an Asian cuisine. This recipe of a fruit salad would be perfect as a re-fresher. It can be also used as a light dessert.

The selection of fruits is up to your preference. The fruits suggested here can be used as an example.

Ingredients

1 medium ripe mango, sliced (5 oz.)
1 medium ripe banana, sliced (4 1/2 oz.)
3/4-1 cup halved strawberry (6 oz.)
1 medium apple, chopped into 1 pieces (4 oz.)
3 tbsp. sugar substitute or sugar
1/4 tsp Chinese five spice powder
1/4 tsp vanilla extract
1 tsp lemon juice

Process

Combine all in a bowl and mix, or cover and shake to mix. Let it marinate for a few hours in the refrigerator.

Keep in refrigerator until serving.
Note: Bananas may turn brown

Sophia Dediu — Dim Sum

ICEBERG LETTUCE SOUP

Ingredients

3 cups iceberg lettuce, sliced in long threads
2 slices fresh ginger, each the size of a 25-cent piece, julienned
1 tbsp. peanut oil
1/4 tsp salt
4 cups chicken stock (or veggie stock)
1 tbsp. Chinese rice wine or 1 tablespoon dry sherry

Garnish
sesame oil
white pepper, to taste

Process

Thinly slice the boneless fish and soak in the marinade.
Shred the lettuce and set aside.

Cook the ginger, oil and salt just until the ginger begins to brown a little bit. Add to the soup stock and bring to a heavy simmer.

Just prior to serving, drain the marinade from the fish and add the fish to the soup pot, all at once, along with the lettuce and the rice wine or sherry.
Bring back to a full simmer, and then remove from stove.

Do not overcook the soup.
Add a few drops of sesame oil and pepper for garnish, and serve immediately.

Sophia Dediu — Dim Sum

DIM SUM POT STICKERS
Ingredients

---

gyoza skins (dim sum wrappers) or any other

water or broth, for sealing and steaming
cornstarch, for sealing
peanut oil (for frying)

Filling
1 tbsp. lb. ground chicken (read *NOTE) or 1 lb. ground lean pork (read *NOTE)
2 tbsp. tamari
1 tbsp. sherry wine or 1 tablespoon rice wine
1/2 tsp sugar
2 -3 green onions, sliced thinly
1 tsp freshly grated ginger
2 garlic cloves, finely minced
1 carrot, peeled and minced
1 tsp regular sesame oil
1 egg, slightly beaten
1 tbsp. cornstarch

Dipping Sauce
1/4 cup tamari
1/4 cup rice vinegar
1/2 tsp freshly grated ginger
1/2 tsp toasted sesame oil
3 slices green onions

Process

Dipping sauce:
In a small non-reactive bowl combine the dipping sauce and set aside to marinate. Best prepared several hours in advance.

Sophia Dediu Dim Sum

Meat filling:
In a large bowl combine the filling ingredients. Cover and refrigerate at least 1 hour.

To make a simple paste for sealing the wrappers, in another small bowl combine a few tablespoons of water and roughly 1 teaspoon cornstarch. Stir to blend. Place about 3/4 tablespoon of the meat mixture on one dim sum wrapper. Using your fingers or a pastry brush, add a little bit of the water/cornstarch mixture to the edge of the wrapper. Fold over the wet edges so they meet and they should look like mini-turnovers. Be sure edges are sealed firmly so that the dim sum do not fall apart during cooking.

(If you own a dim sum wrapper maker use that. If you don't own one, considering investing in a dim sum wrapper. They are inexpensive and come in very handy! A small turnover maker will also work.).
Place the filled dim sum singly on parchment or waxed paper lined cookie sheet. Fill all the dim sum wrappers.

Frying the Dim Sum: In large sauté pan, on medium-high heat the peanut oil, approximately 1 tablespoon. Add the dim sum in batches, DO NOT crowd, and fry until golden on both sides, about 5 minutes.
Once golden, add 1/4 cup of broth or water, cover pan and bring to boil. Reduce heat to simmer and cook for about 20 minutes or until liquid is evaporated and dim sum are tender but not gummy.

Sophia Dediu — Dim Sum

Serve immediately.

Steaming the Dim Sum: Place a large bamboo steamer inside a large stock pot. Fill with water so that the water does not exceed the bottom of the first level or tier of the steamer basket. Lightly oil the inside of the bamboo steamer basket so that the gyozas do not stick. Arrange the dim sum singly in the bamboo steamer, cover and bring water to boil. FYI- Don't put the cover on the stock pot, only the bamboo steamer.

Reduce heat to low-medium and cook for about 20 minutes or until dim sum are tender but not gummy. Make sure the water does not evaporate, checking periodically and adding more if necessary. Serve hot.

Serve the Dim Sum with your favorite dipping sauces.

The meat mixture can be prepared in advance and frozen until ready to use. Any leftover meat mixture can also be placed in the freezer for later use.

Sophia Dediu — Dim Sum
BEEF TENDERLOIN WITH ASPARAGUS

Ingredients

12 oz. asparagus
16 oz. beef tenderloin
4 oz. jasmine rice
1/2 cup Soy Teriyaki Marinade & Sauce
3 tbsp. honey
2 tsp. salt
1 tbsp. olive oil

Process

1. Cook rice according to package directions.
2. Pour 8 cups of water and 2 tsp. of salt in a large saucepot over medium-high heat.
3. Remove the tough ends from the asparagus and discard. Set the asparagus aside.
4. Pat dry the beef tenderloins with paper towels. Season each with 1/4 tsp. of salt and pepper on both sides.
5. Meanwhile, heat 1 Tbsp. of olive oil in a large non-stick sauté pan over medium-high heat.
2. When hot, add the beef tenderloins and sear on both sides for 5 min.
3. Pour teriyaki sauce into a small sauté pan and place over high heat. When it begins to boil, reduce heat to low and simmer until the sauce has thickened and reduced by half, about 3–4 min. Stir in the honey.
4. Place the asparagus in the boiling water and cook for approx. 4 min. The spears should bend slightly.
5. While the asparagus is cooking, slice the beef tenderloins against the grain into equal sized pieces.
6. Arrange the asparagus and beef onto two plates, and spoon the teriyaki reduction around the beef. Serve the rice on the side.

TERIYAKI SALMON WITH KALE AND BROCCOLI
Ingredients

4 salmon fillets (about 6 ounces each)
1/2 cup Soy Teriyaki Marinade & Sauce
1 bunch baby broccoli
1/2 bunch lacinato kale
3 cloves garlic
1/2 cup olive oil
salt & pepper to taste
1 lemon
red pepper flakes to taste

Process
1. Place the salmon fillets in a casserole dish. Pour the Teriyaki sauce over top and turn the fish until evenly coated.
2. Cover with plastic wrap and place in the fridge to marinate for 1 hour.
3. When the salmon is ready, discard any leftover marinade.
4. Preheat the oven to 425°F. Adjust the rack to the center of the oven.
5. Line a baking sheet with foil or parchment paper.

Cook
1. Place the broccoli, kale and garlic on the baking sheet.
2. Drizzle with olive oil and season with salt and pepper. Toss to coat.
3. Nestle the salmon fillets between the vegetables and cook for 15 minutes, or until the vegetables are tender and the salmon is cooked through.
4. Zest the lemon over the salmon and vegetables.
5. Sprinkle lightly with red pepper flakes before serving.

Sophia Dediu   Dim Sum

CHINESE SEAWEED

One of the things I enjoy greatly in Chinese restaurants is Chinese 'seaweed' that often comes with dim sum starters.

I realize that the seaweed is actually stir-fried shredded cabbage and I have managed to make a very acceptable version at home but what I need to find out what the powder that is sprinkled on top is.
I discovered that it is prawn, dried, finely shredded/powdered prawn.

The way I cook it is to finely shred any type of cabbage (though the dark green savoy type seems to be best) and then stir fry it in small quantities in a very hot wok with some shredded ginger (a spoonful or so). It is important to cook it until it starts to go brown (i.e. just before it burns) otherwise it cooks but stays soggy. I then lay it on kitchen paper to drain some of the fat off.

Dried Prawns

A prawn is an edible sea animal resembling a shrimp, with a slender body, a long tail, five pairs of legs, and two pairs of pincers. Genera: Palaemon Penaeus. The powder is "prawn powder". This is made by roasting equal quantities of dried prawns and pran shells in a hot oven for 10-15 minutes and then grinding the result down to a powder.

Many Chinese restaurants will serve their own form of dim sum as a 'house' specialty, and it's hard to guess what was used.

Sophia Dediu — Dim Sum

CHINESE STYLE RIBS

Ingredients

2 - 3 lbs. baby back ribs
1/3 cup soy sauce
1/3 cup honey
3 tbsp. white vinegar
2 tbsps cooking sherry
1 tbsps ginger
3 cloves chopped garlic
1 ½ cups beef broth

Process

Mix all ingredients and stir well. Add ribs and marinate at least 3 hours.
Place ribs on rack in roasting pan and bake at 350º F for 1 to 1 1/2 hours till brown and crispy. Baste often.

Sophia Dediu — Dim Sum

BARBEQUE SPARERIBS

Ingredients

2 sides of pork ribs halved lengthwise
1 quart Cola
½ cup soy sauce
½ cup Cream Sherry

Process

Make the marinade by combining the liquid ingredients and pour over the ribs. Let stand 2 hours. Bake at 350º F for 45 to 50 minutes, basting frequently until the ribs are shiny and crisp.

SWEET CHINESE STYLE RIBS

Here is a recipe the mother of my friend used to make when she was a kid.

Cut the ribs up or separate them. Then wash them, and put them in a pot.

Measure enough water just to cover, usually about two cups of water per pound.

Then use double of the amount of water in brown sugar; example: if you use 4 cups of water then you need 2 cups of brown sugar, lots of crushed garlic about 4 cloves and about a quarter of a cup soy sauce (if your soy sauce is light in color you might need more).

Then simmer for about 2 to 2 and one half hours on medium low with the lid open a bit, or until desired thickness.

In the end the meat starts to fall of the bone.
Finger liking good ribs!

Sophia Dediu   Dim Sum

RICE RINGS

Boil your rice as usual. When it's done thoroughly rinse; put it in a mixing bowl and add salt, pepper, a little five spice, some finely chopped red pepper and bind it all together with an egg. Take the mixture and on a greased tray make rings of the rice about the size of a cup.

Put the rings under a hot grill until the rings are firm and the tops are just lightly browning (the egg not the rice). Serve them while they're hot.

According to Confucius (Kong Qui) a person well-educated would
- speak carefully and modestly;
- be resolute and firm, courageous;
- free from worry, unhappiness, and insecurity;
- moderate their desires;
- be respectful, tolerant, diligent, trustworthy and kind;
- love others.

Sophia Dediu — Dim Sum

CHILI TOFU WITH CAPSICUM

Here's a popular dish in Nanjing (China).
The Chinese name is Tsa Tsa Mien.

Ingredients

---

1 Tub fresh tofu
1 green capsicum/pepper/paprika (whatever you want to call them)
1 red capsicum/pepper/paprika
1 white onion
3 red chili
5 dried mushrooms soaked in water
Ginger
Garlic
Arrowroot/corn flour
Soy sauce
Rice vinegar
A little oyster sauce

Process

Chop onions and capsicum into 2cm squares, chop roughly chili, garlic and ginger, and soak the mushroom in warm water. Mix arrowroot/corn flour, soy, vinegar and oyster sauce (I think you can use something else for this, it's mainly the color that's important, and perhaps some stock

Fry off onions, chili and capsicums, add mushrooms, ginger and garlic

add blob of tofu, and mix up/chop with spatula, add sauce ingredients and mix until tofu looks like scrambled eggs.

It was also served with a cucumber and tomato salad beforehand.
Chop cucumber (Lebanese type cucumber) into 10cm length strips, crush about 6 cloves of garlic and put on top with some salt, sprinkle sesame oil and soy sauce over top.

I found leaving the garlic in the soy sauce overnight adds even more flavor.

At Perking Garden in Lexington, they serve a dish at lunch time called Peking Noodles. It looks like a Chinese spaghetti dish, but the sauce is dark brown and uses pork instead of beef.

Sophia Dediu   Dim Sum

TSA CHIANG MEIN (PEKING MEAT SAUCE NOODLES)
Ingredients

1 lb. lean pork, minced (or ground)
1/4 cup (or less) vegetable oil
½ cup bean sauce
2 tbsp. hoisin sauce
½ tsp white pepper
2 scallions, finely chopped
3-4 tsp sugar
Cooked noodles
Bean sprouts, shredded radishes, shredded cucumber for garnish

Process

1. Heat oil in wok. The exact amount of oil you need will depend on how fatty the pork is and how oily you want the dish to be. The Peking Garden style is sparing on the oil. You need enough for the pork to fry properly. I've found that if you use normal (not extra-lean) ground pork, the pork itself has enough fat that you don't need any added oil.
2. Add pork and stir fry 3 minutes, until all pinkness is gone.
3. Add bean sauce and hoisin sauce. Stir-fry 2 minutes.
4. Add sugar and white pepper. Cook 3 minutes.
5. Add scallions and stir to blend.
6. To serve, place a portion of noodles in a bowl then place some of the garnishes as they wish over the noodles, then spoon on a few tbsp. of the meat sauce.

Addendum:
The recipe from one of the Chinese cookbooks I have. I've found that you get something closer to what they serve in Chinese restaurants in New England if, before you add the pork, you stir-fry a chopped small onion in a bit of oil.

As bean sauce I use the Koon Chun brand, the kind that has soy bean halves in it. This is what they label simply as "bean sauce". I prefer it to the "ground bean sauce" (or miso), because it isn't as salty and therefore works better in this dish.

ROAST PORK BUNS (BAO BUNS)

Ingredients

Roast pork
1/4 cup firmly packed brown sugar
1/4 cup ketchup
2 tbsp. soy sauce
2 tbsp. hoisin sauce
1 tbsp. dry sherry
1 garlic clove, minced
1 ½ pounds pork steaks (1/2-inch thick)
Sauce:
1 tbsp. cornstarch
1 tbsp. dry sherry
1 tbsp. peanut oil
½ cup chopped onion
½ cup chopped water chestnuts
1 tbsp. soy sauce
1 tbsp. hoisin sauce
½ cup chicken broth
1 (17.3-ounce) can Pillsbury Grands Refrigerated Buttermilk Biscuits
Glaze:
1 tsp sugar
1 tsp water
1 egg white

Process

Heat the oven to 375 degrees. Line a broiler pan with foil. In blender container or food processor, combine all roast pork ingredients except pork. Blend until smooth. Generously brush both sides of the pork steaks, reserving the remaining sauce. Place the pork steaks on the foil-line pan; bake 30 minutes. Brush both sides of pork with remaining sauce and bake 10 to 20 minutes more until tender. Let cool. Finely chop the meat.

In a small bowl, combine cornstarch and sherry. Blend well. Heat the oil in a wok and stir-fry onion and water chestnuts until the onion begins to brown. Add soy and hoisin; stir to coat. Add the chicken broth and stir in the cornstarch mixture. Cook and stir until thickened. Remove from heat; stir in pork.

Sophia Dediu   Dim Sum

Separate the dough into 8 biscuits. Press or roll each into a 5-inch circle on a lightly floured surface. Place about 1/3 cup of the pork mixture in the center and gather up the edges, pinch and twist to seal. Place seam side down on an ungreased cookie sheet. In a small bowl, beat the glaze ingredients until blended; brush over buns. Bake at 375º F until golden brown.
Makes 8 sandwiches.

Sophia Dediu   Dim Sum

SWEET AND SOUR SAUCE

Here's a bulk standard sweet and sour sauce I once got from a restaurant owner.

Ingredients

A little orange juice,
Apple juice and
Lemon juice
Lots of Chinese red wine vinegar (it smells of five spice and is a nice pink color)
Arrowroot flour (as it's clearer than corn flour)
Sugar
Either veggie/chicken stock or plain water (to make up half the volume)
A little ground pepper (usually white)
A drizzle of sesame oil (say about 10g)

Process

Add all together; cook until thickened and a the a few seconds longer to cook the starch out.

105

Sophia Dediu   Dim Sum

CHOP SOEY
Ingredients

3 lbs. pork (cubed)
1 cup oil
1 large bunch celery (chopped)
6 or 7 green peppers (chopped)
1-2 large or several small onions (chopped)
2-3 lbs. bean sprouts (fresh)
La choy soy sauce
Salt and pepper

Process

Note:
Use a cheap pork roast (butt) not too lean; it's better for this dish. Also, the vegetables should not be chopped too small. In a very large pot, sauté pork in oil until brown. Add celery and mix in. Chop the rest of vegetables. Add peppers and onions, cook till almost tender. Add bean sprouts, cover and cook for about another 1/2- 3/4 hour until everything is tender and the liquid reaches the top of vegetables.

Do not add any water to this dish even if when you add the sprouts it seems that more water is needed. While mixing the sprouts these will release the necessary
Add soy sauce to taste.

Sophia Dediu   Dim Sum

CHICKEN CHOW MEIN

This is my good friend Juliana's recipe for chicken chow-mein. It is not true authentic chow-mein but it sure tastes good. It is easy to make and is great with leftover chicken or turkey.

Ingredients

---

6 tbsp. cooking oil
2 cups chopped onion
2 cups thin sliced celery
4 cups cooked and slivered chicken
8 oz. can mushrooms, sliced
2 cans water chestnuts, sliced
5 tbsp. cornstarch
½ cup cold water
2 ½ cups strong soup stock
2 tsp salt
½ tsp pepper
2 tsp sugar
3 tbsp. molasses
2 cans bean sprouts
1 large can crunchy chow-mein noodles (La Choy)

Process

Sauté the onion, celery in oil about 10 minutes. Add chicken, mushrooms, water chestnuts and soy sauce.

Add soup stock salt, pepper, sugar. Add thickening or cornstarch dissolved in cold water. Add molasses and cook. Add sprouts and cook 10 minutes more before serving. Serve over chow Mein noodles.

She said that this is her father's recipe which always went over very big at his hunting and club functions. Hope you enjoy.

Forgot to tell you that this will probably need to be thickened a little after you add the soy sauce. I use corn starch.

CABBAGE ROLLS
Ingredients

12 leaves cabbage
1 cup cooked white rice
1 egg, beaten
1/4 cup milk
1/4 cup minced onion
1 pound extra-lean ground beef
1 1/4 teaspoons salt
1 1/4 teaspoons ground black pepper
1 (8 ounce) can tomato sauce
1 tbsp. brown sugar
1 tbsp. lemon juice
1 tsp Worcestershire sauce

Process

Bring a large pot of water to a boil. Boil cabbage leaves for two minutes; drain
In large a bowl, combine 1 cup cooked rice, egg, milk, onion, ground beef, salt, and pepper. Place about 1/4 cup of meat mixture in center of each cabbage leaf, and roll up, tucking in ends. Place rolls in slow cooker.
In a small bowl, mix together tomato sauce, brown sugar, lemon juice, and Worcestershire sauce. Pour over cabbage rolls.
Cover, and cook on low 8 to 9 hours.

CHINESE GREEN BEANS

Very quick and simple to make.

Ingredients

1 lb. fresh green beans
vegetable oil cooking spray or
2 tablespoons peanut oil
1 tsp gingerroot, peeled, minced
1 garlic clove, minced
2 tbsp. water
1 tbsp. soy sauce
1 tsp cornstarch
1/2 tsp brown sugar
1/2 tsp sesame oil
1/4 tsp crushed red pepper flakes

Process

Wash beans, trim ends and remove strings.
Arrange beans in a vegetable steamer (or a colander that will sit nicely in saucepan), and place over boiling water.
Cover and steam 5 minutes.
Drain and plunge into cold water, drain again.
Coat a large nonstick skillet (or wok) with cooking spray or peanut oil and heat until hot.

Add gingerroot and garlic and sauté for half a minute
Add beans, sauté 5 minutes.
Combine 2 tablespoons water and remaining 5 ingredients.
Stir well.
Add to the beans, cook 30 seconds or until thoroughly heated, stirring constantly.

Sophia Dediu — Dim Sum

AUTHENTIC CHINESE FRIED RICE

The classic Chinese seasonings are: garlic, ginger, sherry or rice wine, and some soy sauce. Without them, it's not Chinese fried rice, period.

Ingredients

2 cups instant rice
2 cups water
1/2 medium onion, diced
1/4 cup frozen mixed peas and carrots (doesn't have to be thawed)
1/4 cup soy sauce (sounds like a lot, but it IS 2 cups of rice!)
1 egg
4 tbsp. oil, divided

Process

In a small pot, bring the water to a boil and then stir in rice. Cover with a tight-fitting lid and set aside.

In a large skillet, place 2 tablespoons of oil to get hot over med-high heat. Scramble egg, stir-frying and make sure are well broken up. Put it into your serving bowl and set aside.

Put the other two tablespoons of oil in the skillet and fry the onion until almost transparent. Add the peas and carrots, stir-frying those to thaw. Heat thoroughly.

In the meantime, the rice should be ready; pour it into the skillet and add the egg. Pour in the soy sauce.

Toss all ingredients over med-high heat and stir quickly. Until the rice and all the soy sauce is distributed and the color and strength is to your liking.

Serve it with your favorite other Chinese dishes or it can be served alone as a dish.

Sophia Dediu   **Dim Sum**

Sophia Dediu   Dim Sum

CHINESE STYLE KALE

This is a way to make the bitterness of the kale more palatable

Ingredients

1 tbsp. vegetable oil
1 large garlic clove, sliced
7 ounces kale
3 fluid ounces boiling water
1 tbsp. soy sauce
1 tbsp. oyster sauce

Process

Heat the oil in a large wok or frying pan. Make sure is not burning hot.
Add in the garlic and cook for a few seconds.
Add in the kale and toss around the pan to coat in the garlicky oil.
Pour over boiling water and cook for seven minutes or until the kale gets wilted and is cooked through.
Lastly, stir in the soy and oyster sauces and heat through and serve.

Sophia Dediu   Dim Sum

CHINESE DUMPLINGS

The good thing about dumplings is that there are so many kinds of dumpling. Most people prefer boiled dumplings over steamed dumplings. Some restaurants specialize in dumplings and that is the only thing on their menu.
This is an authentic recipe given to me by a friend.

It is recommended to double the ingredients because they'll be gone in no time.

For the dough you can use wonton wrappers, which you'll have to roll them thinner.

Ingredients

Dough
2 cups flour
2 eggs, large
2 tbsp. vegetable oil
1/2 cup cold water, divided

Filling
3/4 cup Chinese chives (find these in an Asian market, you could substitute regular chives or scallions, but it won't be qui)
1 lb. ground pork
1 tsp soy sauce
1 tbsp. cornstarch
1 tsp ginger juice (I grate some ginger and press it in a garlic press)
1/2 tsp chicken bouillon powder
1 tsp sesame oil
1/2 tsp finely minced garlic
salt & pepper

Process

Dough
Place flour in a bowl and make a well.
Lightly whisk the eggs in a separate bowl.
Mix together the eggs, oil, and half the water to make a dough. Add more water as needed. The dough should not be sticky
Knead the dough on a floured surface for about ten minutes.
Cover and set it aside to rest for half hour.

Sophia Dediu   Dim Sum

Filling
Mix the rest of the ingredients in a bowl. Do not overmix the meat, it should remain fluffy.
Cover the bowl and refrigerate for half hour to give time for flavors to blend.

Assemble:
Roll out the dough into thin sheets. Make sure that the sheets are not too thin because they'll brake easily.
Use a large round cookie cutter and cut out the rounds.
Each round gets filled with one tablespoon of the meat mixture. Damp the edges of the filled rounds with water and then seal.

Cook
Steam the dumplings for 12 minutes.
You can serve them as they come out from the steamer or you can stir-fry them in a little peanut oil just until they get a little crispy.
Serve them with your favorite dipping sauces.
If you want to store some of them you have to cool them off first and then place them in a zip bag and refrigerate for up to 3 days.

Sophia Dediu   **Dim Sum**

Sophia Dediu — Dim Sum

CHINESE TEA EGGS (TAIWAN)

In Taiwan, this is a side street snack any time of the day.
These eggs can also be sliced and served along with other cold cuts.

Ingredients

8 eggs
water
3 tbsp. salt (can be quite liberal with salt)
2 tbsp. s Chinese five spice powder
1 star anise
1 tea bag (any kind of plain black tea)

Process

Bring the eggs to a boil and simmer for 3-5 minutes.
Drain and cool.
When cool enough to handle, gently crack the egg's shell all over without removing the shell.

Place the eggs back in the pan, cover the eggs with water, add the remaining ingredients and bring back to boil, then reduce the heat and have them simmer for an hour. In this time the tea flavor infuses the eggs.

Drain the eggs.
The eggs can be served cold or warm.

Sophia Dediu — Dim Sum

CHINESE BODDHA'S DELIGHT
Ingredients

3 tbsp. low sodium soy sauce
1 tbsp. dark sesame oil
1 tbsp. rice vinegar
1 tsp sugar
1(14 ounce) package water-packed extra firm tofu, drained and cut into 1-inch cubes
5 cups small broccoli florets
1 1/2cups carrots (1/4-inch diagonally sliced)
1/2cup peeled chopped broccoli stem
2 tbsp. canola oil
1 1/2cups sliced green onions
1 tbsp. grated peeled fresh ginger
2 garlic cloves, minced
1 cup snow peas, trimmed
1(14 ounce) can whole baby corn, drained
1(8 ounce) can sliced water chestnuts, drained
1/2 cup vegetable broth
1 tbsp. cornstarch
1/2 tsp salt
4 cups hot cooked brown rice

Process

Combine first 5 ingredients, tossing to coat.
Cover and marinate in refrigerator 1 hour.
Drain in a colander over a bowl, reserving marinade.
Cook broccoli florets, carrot, and broccoli stems in boiling water 1 1/2 minutes.
Drain these vegetables.
Plunge into ice water.
Drain.

Heat canola oil in a wok or large nonstick skillet over medium-high heat.
Add tofu.
Stir-fry for 5 minutes or until lightly browned on all sides.

Sophia Dediu   Dim Sum

Stir in the onions, ginger, and garlic.
Stir-fry for 30 seconds.

Stir in the broccoli mixture, snow peas, corn, and water chestnuts.
Stir-fry for one minute.

Combine the broth and cornstarch, stirring with a whisk.
Add cornstarch mixture, reserved marinade, and salt to pan.
Bring them to a boil.
Cook for two and half minutes or until slightly thick, stirring constantly.
Serve over brown or on an type of rice.

Chinese proverb about money:

With money you can buy a house, but you cannot buy a home,
With money you can buy a watch, but you cannot buy time,
With money you can buy a bed, but you cannot buy rest
With money you can buy a book, but you cannot buy culture,
With money you can buy a doctor, but you cannot buy health,
With money you can buy a position, but you cannot buy respect,
With money you can buy blood, but you cannot buy life
With money you can buy sex, but you cannot buy love.

Sophia Dediu — Dim Sum

CHINESE ALMOND COOKIES

Ingredients

3 cups flour
1 cup sugar
1/2 tsp baking soda
1/2 teaspoon salt
1/4 tsp cinnamon
1 1/2 cups shortening
1 egg, beaten
1 tsp almond extract
72 sliced almonds, or whole

Process

Preheat oven to 350 degrees F.

Sift flour with sugar, soda salt and cinnamon into a large bowl or food processor by pulsing 3-4 times. Mix in shortening and knead thoroughly (8 to 10 minutes by hand 60 second to 1 minute with food processor).

Combine egg and almond extract; stir into flour mixture. Mix well.
Shape into balls using 1 tablespoon of dough.

Place on ungreased baking sheets and make a depression in the top with the thumb. Press a blanched whole or sliced almond into the center of each cookie. Bake for 15 to 18 minutes.
Makes six dozen.

OTHER CHINESE ALMOND COOKIES

Ingredients

2 3/4 cups sifted all-purpose flour
1 cup white sugar
1/2 tsp baking soda
1/2 tsp salt
1 cup lard
1 egg
1 tsp almond extract
28 almonds

Process

1. Preheat oven to 325 degrees F (165 degrees C).
2. Sift flour, sugar, baking soda and salt together into a bowl. Cut in the lard until mixture resembles cornmeal. Add egg and almond extract. Mix well.
3. Roll dough into 1-inch balls. Set them 2 inches apart on an ungreased cookie sheet. Place an almond on top of each cookie and press down to flatten slightly.
4. Bake in the preheated oven until the edges of the cookies are golden brown, 15 to 18 minutes.

Sophia Dediu   Dim Sum

CHINESE BRUSSELS SPROUTS

Ingredients

2 cups Brussels sprouts, quartered
2 minced garlic cloves
1/2 inch piece ginger, peeled and sliced
1/2 onion, sliced thin
1/2 teaspoon red pepper flakes (to taste)
slurry soy sauce, cornstarch, sugar and sesame oil

Process

Stir fry sprouts in hot oil with garlic, onion and ginger until nearly done (about 3 min.). Mix slurry ingredients together and add to sprouts. Sprinkle with crushed red pepper. Stir-fry for 2 minutes more. Serve hot with Char Siu Ribs and Steamed Rice.

Sophia Dediu — Dim Sum

MEAN CHINESE CHICKEN LO MEIN
Ingredients

lb. linguine
1/2lb chicken (sliced 1/8 in. thick)
1tsp cornstarch
1 tbsp. light soy sauce
1 tsp sherry wine
1/2 tsp garlic (crushed)

Sauce Mixture
1 tbsp. cornstarch
1 cup chicken broth
1 tbsp. light soy sauce
2 tbsp. oyster sauce
1 tsp sesame tbsp. e oil
1 stalk green onion (diced)
2 tbsp. vegetable oil

Process

Par boil linguine noodles for about 3 minute.
Rinse with cold water and drain.
Marinate chicken for 15 minute in 1tsp cornstarch 1 tbsp. light soy sauce and 1 tsp sherry.

Prepare a pot of hot water and heat your wok.
Add 2 tbsp. vegetable oil and reheat.

Add garlic; brown and discard he garlic.
Add chicken and the marinade.
Stir until 3/4 done.

Add the sauce mixture and stir until thickens.
Note:
The thickening agents will be completely done when the mixture boils for approximately1 minute.

Add green onions and sesame oil. Mix well and keep warm.
Drop noodles into hot water and stir to heat.
Drain well and add to meat and sauce in the wok mixing well.

Sophia Dediu   Dim Sum

Sophia Dediu — Dim Sum

CHINESE KUNG PAO CHICKEN
Ingredients

1 lb. boneless skinless chicken breast
1 egg white
1 tablespoon cornstarch
1 dash white pepper
1 tsp soy sauce

Vegetables
8 medium Thai peppers (as many as you like, I use about 8)
1 large green pepper, cut into bite size squares (leave them out if you don't like them)
1 medium onion, cut into bite size pieces (if you leave out the peppers, perhaps increase the onions)
2 stalks celery, cut into bite size pieces on the diagonal
1
(8 ounce) can sliced water chestnuts, drained

Sauce
4 tbsp. soy sauce
2 tbsp. dry sherry
2 tbsp. rice wine vinegar
2 tbsp. sugar
2 tsp sesame oil
2 -3 tbsp. hoisin sauce
2 -3 tbsp. oyster sauce
1 tbsp. peanut oil
1/2 cup roasted unsalted peanuts

Process

Cut chicken into bite size pieces.
Combine egg white, corn starch, pepper and soy sauce in a glass bowl. Add chicken pieces mixing to coat well. Cover and refrigerate 30 minutes.

Sauce:
Mix all sauce ingredients in a glass bowl and set aside.

In a wok or large frying pan, stir fry the red peppers in the 1 tbsp. peanut oil over medium-high heat until the peppers are almost golden brown.

Add chicken mixture and stir-fry until the chicken is almost cooked through-add the vegetables and stir-fry a couple of minutes.

Add the sauce mixture and heat for a minute or so.
Serve over rice and sprinkle peanuts over each serving.

CHINESE GINGER RICE
Ingredients

1 cup short-grain rice
1/2 tsp fresh ginger, finely minced
1/2tsp toasted sesame oil
2 cups water
1/2tsp salt

Process

Rinse the rice in a strainer and drain.
In a saucepan, heat the oil and sauté the ginger over medium heat until fragrant, about one to two minutes.

Stir in the rice. Add the water and salt and bring it to a boil.
Reduce the heat and let it simmer covered until the water is absorbed, about 12-15 minutes.
Stir it once and give it a rest until ready to serve.

CHINESE LION'S HEAD SOUP

Ingredients

1 pound ground pork
1 egg
1 tbsp. cornstarch
2 tsp sesame oil
1 tbsp. minced fresh ginger root
1/4 tsp monosodium glutamate (MSG) (optional)
1 tsp salt
2 green onions, chopped and divided
1 tbsp. vegetable oil
1 head Napa cabbage, cored and cut into chunks
2 cups low-sodium chicken broth
2 cups water, or as needed
1 tbsp. soy sauce
2 tsp sesame oil

Process

Mix the ground pork with the egg, cornstarch, sesame oil, ginger, monosodium glutamate, salt, and half of the chopped green onions in a bowl. Set aside.

Heat the vegetable oil in a wok or large skillet over high heat. When the oil is hot, fry the Napa cabbage, stirring constantly, until cabbage begins to wilt, 2 to 3 minutes. Pour in the chicken broth, water, and soy sauce. Bring to a boil, and then lower the heat to medium.

Use a spoon to form the meat mixture into one inch balls. Drop them into the boiling soup. Cover with a lid and simmer for 10 minutes.
Season with salt before serving. Garnish with remaining green onions and optional a drizzle of sesame oil.

Sophia Dediu   Dim Sum

CHINESE SOOP SHAZAMI

This is a quick, easy and tasty soup. It is low in calories and delicious base soup. You can add different vegetables.

Ingredients

6 cups water or 6 cups chicken stock
2 tbsp. chicken bouillon powder (reduce to 1/2 tsp if you use stock)
1 carrot, grated
2 cups cabbage, thinly sliced
1/2 onion, finely chopped
1 tbsp. fresh ginger or 1 1/2 teaspoons dried ginger
1 garlic clove, diced
1 1/2 teaspoons sesame oil (or more to taste)
1/2 tsp white pepper (or more to taste)

Process

Put water and bullion in a pot and turn heat on high.
Grate a carrot, finely slice cabbage leaving the strips long, finely dice onion and place them in the pot.
Pill the bark off of a 1/2 inch piece of fresh ginger and then chop it very finely adding it to the pot.
Add also the garlic.
After the soup comes to a boil, reduce the heat and simmer for about 20 minutes or until veggies are soft.
Add sesame oil and white pepper and stir.

Sophia Dediu   Dim Sum

CHINESE BAKED SWEET BREAD DOUGH

The Chinese bread dough is sweeter in comparison with the Western breads. Most common Chinese breads are steamed. Traditionally, in the south parts of Chine the bread is quite sweet. The bread can be made plain or used for Chinese buns (bao), which are filled with a variety of fillings, such as custard, bean paste, or meat.

Ingredients

1 tbsp. active dry yeast (1 package)
3 tbsp. sugar
1 cup warm milk (about 100 to 110 degrees F)
1 egg
3/4 cup vegetable oil
3 1/2 cups all-purpose flour, and more for dusting and kneading

Process

In a small bowl put the yeast, one tsp of sugar and 1/4 cup of the warm milk. After 5 minutes it should foam and bubble.
Stir in the egg, oil and the remaining milk.

In a large bowl of the food processor place the flour and remaining sugar. Process for 2 seconds. While the machine is running, pour the warm milk mixture down in a steady stream. Process until it forms a rough ball. If ball is sticky and wet, add a little more flour. Process a few seconds longer, or until dough pulls away from the sides of the bowl.

Remove dough to a lightly floured board. Knead the dough, dusting with flour to keep it from sticking, until becomes smooth and elastic, about 2 minutes.
Place in a large oiled bowl, cover with plastic wrap and let it rise for about one hour in a warm spot until doubled.

Punch down dough and place it on a lightly floured surface. Now you start to form it into rolls, buns or loaves.

Preparing filled buns
Cut the dough in half. Form each half into a 12-inch long log; cut it into 10 pieces. Roll each piece into a 4-inch circle. Roll outer inch of each circle 1/8-inch thin; leave middle slightly thicker.

Sophia Dediu   Dim Sum

Process
1. If right-handed, place a dough circle in your left hand palm;
2. Place a tablespoon of filling in the middle;
3. Put the left thumb over the filling.
4. With your right hand, bring up edge and make a pleat in it.
5. Rotate the dough circle a little and make a second pleat.
6. As you make each pleat, gently pull it up and around as if to enclose your thumb.
7. Continue rotating, pleating and pinching, then gently twist into a spiral. Pinch to seal.
8 Place bun pleated side down on a parchment square. Repeat with remaining dough and filling.
9. Put buns 1 1/2 inches apart on a baking sheet. Let rise until doubled in size, 30 minutes to 1 hour.

Preheat oven to 350^0 F. Beat the egg yolks with water and sugar; brush over buns. Bake 20 minutes.

Sophia Dediu   Dim Sum

CHINESE CRISPY SPRING ROLLS

This is a vegetarian version of spring rolls.
You can replace the mushrooms with minced meat if you like a meat version.
Or, if you like shrimp, just add them in the place of carrots.

Ingredients

---

40 spring rolls
1 cup bean sprouts
1 bunch scallion
2 carrots
2/3 cup bamboo shoot, sliced
1 1/2 cups mushrooms
3 -4 tbsp. vegetable oil
1 tsp light brown sugar
1 tbsp. light soy sauce
1 tbsp. rice wine (or dry sherry)
20 egg roll wraps (approx.)
1 tbsp. cornstarch paste
flour (for dusting)
oil (for deep frying)
soy sauce (for dipping, or other dipping sauces, as desired)

Process

Shred all vegetables preferable to the size of the bean sprouts.
Heat 2 tbsp. oil in wok and stir-fry vegetables for 1 minute.
Add salt, sugar, light soy sauce, and rice wine.
Stir-fry 2 minutes more; drain and cool.

To make a spring roll, cut the wrapper in half diagonally.
Place 1 tbsp. of veggie mixture one-third of the way down the wrapper, then turn the wrapper so the small tip of the diagonal is pointing away from you.
Fold the wide edge of the wrapper over the filling and roll over one time.
Fold in the sides, and roll the wrapper away from you one time more.

Brush the upper edge of the wrapper with cornstarch paste (mix 4 parts cornstarch with 5 parts cold water). Finish rolling the spring roll, keeping it a bit tight.
Sprinkle some flour on a baking sheet (to keep spring rolls from sticking), and rest the spring rolls there, flap side down, while you finish making the other rolls.

Sophia Dediu   Dim Sum

To cook, heat the oil in a wok or fryer until hot, and then reduce the heat to low. Fry the spring rolls in batches, making sure not to crowd, cooking until they are golden and crispy, about 2-3 minutes.
Remove rolls from oil and drain on paper toweling.
Serve hot with soy sauce, or sweet and sour and hot mustard.

"What you do not wish for yourself, do not do to others."

Confucius (or honorific Kǒng Fūzǐ – literally "Grand Master Kong")
September 28, 551 BC – 479 BC
Philosopher during the Spring and Autumn period in the Chinese history.

Sophia Dediu — Dim Sum

CHINESE NEW YEAR RICE

Ingredients

3 tbsp. vegetable oil
1 lb. cooked chicken breast, cut into bite-size pieces
3 1/2 cups cooked rice, chilled
3 green onions, sliced
1 stalk celery, diagonally sliced
1 small carrot, shredded
1 -2 tablespoon soy sauce
1/8 tsp black pepper

Process

Heat the oil in a large skillet or wok over medium high heat.
Add chicken.
Cook and stir until lightly browned.
Add remaining ingredients.
Cook and stir about 10 minutes.
Serve.

Sophia Dediu — Dim Sum

GAI LAN - CHINESE BROCCOLI - WITH OYSTER SAUCE

This dish is often served at dim sum restaurants. Gai lan is sometimes referred to as Chinese broccoli.
Note: Do not overcook.

Ingredients

1 lb. gai lan
1 1/2 tbsp. vegetable oil
3 garlic cloves, peeled and smashed
1/4 cup chicken stock
1 tbsp. Chinese rice wine (or sherry)
1/2 tsp sugar
3 tbsp. oyster sauce
3/4 inch fresh ginger, cut into 1/4 inch pieces and smashed
1 tsp sesame oil

Process

Wash the gai lan and trim the ends of stalk and discard.
Mix the chicken stock, rice wine, and sugar in a small bowl and set aside.
In a large wok or pan heat 1 1/2 tbsp. vegetable oil over medium heat. Add the garlic cloves and cook until lightly golden about 1 to 2 minutes. Be careful not to burn the garlic.
Turn the heat to high and add the ginger and cook for 15 to 20 seconds and add gai lan stalks.

With a large spoon or spatula scoop up the oil and bathe the gai lan stalks for about 1 minute.
Pour the chicken stock mixture and immediately cover the wok with a lid.
Turn down the heat to medium and let gai lan steam for about 3-4 minutes. You should be able to easily pierce with the stalks with a fork.
Remove the gai lan to a plate, leaving any remaining stock mixture in the wok and add oyster sauce and sesame oil. Cook for about 1 minute on medium high and pour the sauce over the cooked gai lan and serve.

Sophia Dediu — Dim Sum

CHINESE BABY BOK CHOY

A simple, delicious way to enjoy baby bok choy.

Ingredients

---

10 bunches baby bok choy
1 tbsp. oil (preferable sesame)
1/2 tsp garlic
1/4 cup chicken broth

Process

Clean baby bok choy in cold water several times to get out the sand/dirt. Slice the vegetable in half length-wise.
Heat the oil over medium heat in skillet.
Add the garlic.
Add baby bok choy to skillet, stirring constantly, about 1 minute, until leaves are coated with oil and beginning to wilt.
Add chicken broth and cover pan.
Simmer for 2-3 minutes. Test for doneness with a fork.
Remove from heat.
Place it on the serving dish; you can move some of the broth.

Sophia Dediu — Dim Sum

CHINESE FISH AND LETTUCE SOUP

Ingredients

1 lb. very fresh white fish, boneless fillet, sliced thin (cod or snapper work well)
Marinade
1 tbsp. light soy sauce
1 tbsp. peanut oil
1 pinch white pepper

Soup
3 cups iceberg lettuce, sliced in long threads
2 slices fresh ginger, each the size of a 25-cent piece, julienned
1 tbsp. peanut oil
1/4 tsp salt
4 cups chicken stock (or veggie stock)
1 tbsp. Chinese rice wine or 1 tbsp. dry sherry

Garnish
sesame oil
white pepper, to taste

Process

Thinly slice the boneless fish and soak in the marinade.
Shred the lettuce and set aside.
In a pot cook the ginger, oil and salt just until the ginger begins to brown a little bit.
Add to the soup stock and bring to a heavy simmer.
Just prior to serving, drain the marinade from the fish and add the fish to the soup pot, all at once, along with the lettuce and the rice wine or sherry.
Bring back to a full simmer, and then remove from heat.
Do not overcook the soup.
Add a few drops of sesame oil and pepper for garnish, and serve immediately.

CHINESE LONG NOODLES

Ingredients

2 tsp vegetable oil
2 tbsp. onions, minced
3 tsp fresh ginger, grated and divided
1 garlic clove, minced
1/2 cup soymilk or 1/2 cup milk
1/4 cup creamy peanut butter
1 tsp fresh lemon juice
1 tbsp. dry white wine
1 tbsp. soy sauce
2 tsp cornstarch
1/2 tsp black pepper
8 ounces boneless skinless chicken breasts cut into strips
8 ounces thin spaghetti, uncooked
cooking spray
1/2 cup snow peas, trimmed
1/2 cup carrot, thinly sliced
1/4 tsp salt
1/4 tsp black pepper
1/2 cup green onion, diagonally sliced (scallions)

Process

Prepare the peanut sauce.
Heat 2 tsp oil in a small saucepan over medium high heat.
Add onion, 1 tsp of the grated ginger, and garlic. Saute about 5 minutes until onion is tender.
Stir in the soy milk (or regular milk of your choice), peanut butter and lemon juice until the peanut butter is melted, stirring constantly. Remove from heat and allow cooling.
Prepare the marinade.
Combine the wine, soy sauce, 2 tsp ginger, cornstarch and 1/2 tsp black pepper in a medium bowl. Add chicken pieces and toss. Cover and marinate in the refrigerator at least 30 minutes.
Cook pasta according to package directions, omitting salt and fat. Drain, rinse and set aside.

Sophia Dediu   Dim Sum

Heat a large nonstick skillet, or wok, coated with cooking spray over medium high heat. Add the marinated chicken. Saute, stirring often, 2 minutes or until no longer pink inside.

Add snow peas and carrot and cook 4 minutes, stirring often, until tender crisp. Stir in peanut sauce, salt, and black pepper. Add noodles and toss until heated through.
Remove from heat and sprinkle with green onions.

Sophia Dediu   **Dim Sum**

CHINESE DRONKEN PRAWNS

Ingredients

600 g large shrimp
2 tbsp. oil
1 tbsp. sesame oil
100 g gingerroot, shredded
700 ml Chinese wine
1/2 tsp salt
1 tsp sugar
2 sprigs fresh cilantro

Process

Heat work with both oils.
Stir fry ginger until fragrant.
Add prawns and fry for 1 minute.
Add rice wine and bring to boil. Blend in salt and sugar.
Dish out when prawns are cooked and serve immediately with garnish.

Sophia Dediu   **Dim Sum**

Sophia Dediu   Dim Sum

STREET FOOD

The reason for the following description is to show a couples of similarities between the Chines traditions and some other parts of the world.

One of the most popular snacks is the Jiān bǐng, a Chinese version of the French crêpe.

Jianbing can be traced back to the Eastern Jin Dynasty (316-420 AD). This means that it is well before Marco Polo went to China. There are many tales about what was the determination for preparing this paper thin piece of fried dough. The tradition has been carried on until these days due to its simplicity of ingredients and the short time of preparation.

In Beijing you'll find a stand in many street corners and next to almost every subway station which will sell snacks and freshly prepared Jiān bǐng.

Jiān bǐng literally means shallow-fried thin bread, which has exactly the appearance and the taste of the crepe. The preparation method of the dough is practically alike. The difference is that in non-Chinese cultures the crepes are usually sweet treat for dessert (but in the recent times you see them assembled in savory manner), the Jiān bǐng is a salty-spicy breakfast snack. Jiān bǐng is especially common in the northeast of China where the wheat flour is more common than rice.

The ingredients for Jiān bǐng
The crepe base: usually made from wheat flour.
An egg
Chopped green onion and coriander
Thick soy sauce, dark and salty
Hot sauce optional
Báocuì –a crispy fritter like cracker made of potato dough.
Some stands offer also pickled radish, salted seaweed or ham sausage. In some regions they use corn flour, potato flour or rice flour.

Another snack in many cities is Baba. It resembling a pizza in size and texture. The baba can be sweet or salty.

The salty baba contains minced pork, chives, and heavy amounts of pig lard giving the baba a flaky outer crust.
The baba is an easily transportable snack.
Although, just like our pizza, baba is best eaten when piping hot right out of the Chinese style oven.

Ingredients onto the round flatted dough:
A layer of rose petal jam (méiguī jiàng)
a dash of brown sugar (hóngtáng),
and a smattering of red bean paste (dòushā)
The edges of the dough are folded sealing in the ingredients inside the bun.
The buns are backed in a special frying pan which is heated from above from a hot charcoals fire.
The buns are good, nutritious and easy to pack in travel, or work place.

POST SCRPTOM

Looking at this breath taken photo taken recently in that part of the world we should remind our readers that in China there are still structures build following the millennia old architecture.

Dating back to ancient times, the houses are enclosed structures called Beijing siheyuan buildings. These are structured to house four generations from the same family. These buildings are houses with a courtyard in the center surrounded by four, one-story housing structures, which maximizes the exposure to the sun and provides also privacy.

The structures are traditionally aligned on axis from North to South. According to Feng shui this alignment will provide good fortune.
The main entrance is on the South and opens on a transition space. In the South area there are rooms which serve as kitchen and servants accommodations
Traditionally, the visitors would enter through another passageway before entering the main courtyard.
The main house on the north end, while the east and west sides made up smaller structures, usually for married children and their families

Sophia Dediu   Dim Sum

Built more than a millennium ago in the South East China in the Fujian province there are famous structures called earth houses. A Han group, called Hakka, migrated in these parts to escape the wars from the North. They build these earth houses made of clay with 3-4 floors, in a circular or square design for protection against the invaders.

One of the most interesting styles of Chinese residences, found mostly in the North is the cave dwellings. These are structures dug out of the sides of cliffs or the ground. These houses will maintain good comfortable temperatures in the summer and winter. These structures can be fully or partially underground. Using this unfriendly terrain for building the living spaces will leave the precious flat areas for farming.

In China as in other civilizations from other parts of the world the social and cultural behavior is based on a very old historical existence. Therefore, the traditions carried from a generation to the next are very rich and durable and in many respects different and somehow strange for us the outsiders.
It is desirable that before you get in direct contact with a Chinese environment by travelling or engaging in a conversation or business you need to become familiar with their customs, traditions, culture, and behavior.
The teachings of Confucius are based on five relationships which influenced most of the Chinese society behavior.
The Confucianism teaches that there are the following relationships: Sovereign and non-sovereign, Father and Son, Friend and Friend, Husband and Wife, and Brother and Sister. Based on these relationships the classification of respect is different than in other societies. The good manners demands that these five relationships be respected above all others. The strangers cannot be treated as

one would treat a friend, family member or someone to whom they are related or work for. If you are a stranger do not expect to be treated with respect.
Family members treat each other with veneration and devotion. Business colleagues go to great lengths and spend large amounts of time with their clients to build relationships.

Two other customs in China that affect social behavior in Chinese culture are mianxi meaning face and li meaning sacrifice. Based on these customs the Chinese will restrain from showing or imposing their emotions on others and will avoid confrontation in the name of social harmony.
The Chinese people will consider impolite to voice disagreement and acknowledge conflicts.
Within Chinese society the preservation of the face and sacrificing to be courteous to those with whom you have relationships is valued above all.

The contemporary Chinese society is one in which competition for space and resources is severe. This is due in part to being over-populated and the result of a long, tumultuous and often unstable history.
Customs in China is synonymous with a special attitude towards competition in bargaining for products or getting in line first for the best deal.

That who seeks revenge should dig two graves. – Chinese proverb

Sophia Dediu  Dim Sum

Table of Contents

Editor's Note 3

INTRODUCTION 4

ABOUT THE SPRING FESTIVAL AND TRADITIONAL DIM SUM 9

DIM SUM FOOD MENUS 26

Starts Dim sum foods Year 4712 26

DIM SUM PARTY YEAR 4713 27

    Flaky Moon Cakes 30

    Pot Stickers (Peking Ravioli) 31

    Si Shi Sha Bing (Fluffy Shrimp Cakes) 32

    Congyou Bing (Oily Scallion Cakes) 33

    Ba Bao Fan (Eight Precious Rice Pudding) 34

    Cantonese Turnip Cake 35

    Sheng Ren Bing (Almond Cookies) 36

    Lop Cheung Bow (Sausage Buns) 37

    Cha Siu Bow (Barbecued Pork Buns) 38

    Chinese Bun Dough 39

    Shu Mai (Pork Dumplings) 40

    Glutinous Rice Balls 41

    Fried Wonton 42

    Stuffed Bananas 43

    Pork-Stuffed Mushrooms 44

    Chun Guen (Spring Rolls) 45

    Lo Bo Si Bing (Flaky Turnip Cakes) 46

    Jia Yao Guo (Crunchy Cashews) 47

    Tianzha netao (Sweet Fried Nuts) 48

Sophia Dediu — Dim Sum

Shanghai Pastry Dough 49

Gah Li Gai So Bang (Curried Chicken Pastry) 50

Dai Gut Yau Gok (Good Luck Dumplings) 52

Stuffed Bitter Melon with Fermented Black Beans 53

Winter Melon Soup 55

DIM SOM PARTY YEAR 4714 56

Tianzha netao (Sweet Fried Nuts) 58

Aromatic Spiced Beef 59

Almond Float (Xing Ren Dou Fu) 60

Stuffed Potato Cakes (See Jai Bang) 61

Hot and Sour Soup (Suen Lot Tong) 62

Wonton Soup 63

Sweet Sesame Bows (Ch'iao Gwo) 64

Water Dumplings (Soi Gau) 65

Glazed Walnuts 66

Moon Cakes (Yue Bing) 67

DIM SOM PARTY YEAR 4715 68

Lotus Root Chips 70

Cold Noodles in Sesa 71

Me Sauce 71

Sweet Fried Nuts (Tianzha Netao) 72

Sausage Buns (Lop Cheung Bow) 73

Barbecued Pork Buns (Cha Siu Bow) 74

Almond Cookies (Sheng Ren Bing) 75

Cantonese Turnip Cake (Dzin Lor Bok Goh) 76

Oily Scallion Cakes (Congyou Bing) 77

Sophia Dediu   **Dim Sum**

Glutinous Shao Mai (Luo Mi Shao Mai) 78

Ginger Chicken Wontons 79

Coconut Tarts.. 80

Cantonese Moon Cakes (Yue Bing)....................... 81

Curry Meat Turnovers.. 82

Tea Eggs 83

Steamed Meat Dumplings (Shao Mai) 85

Butterfly cookies (jow wu deep)............................ 86

Sesame cookies (gee ma bang) 87

OTHER RECEPIES 89

    SPICY FROITE SALADE 89

    ICEBERG LETTUCE SOOP... 90

    DIM SOM POT STICKERS 91

    BEEF TENDERLOIN WITH ASPARAGUS......................... 94

    TERIYAKI SALMON WITH KALE AND BROCCOLI 95

    CHINESE SEAWEED.. 96

    CHINESE STYLE RIBS... 97

    BARBEQUE SPARERIBS 98

    SWEET CHINESE STYLE RIBS 99

    RICE RINGS 100

    CHILI TOFO WITH CAPISCOM....................................... 101

    TSA CHIANG MEIN (PEKING MEAT SAUCE NOODLES)...................... 102

    ROAST PORK BUNS (BAO BUNS) 103

    SWEET AND SOUR SAUCE 105

    CHOP SUEY 106

CHICKEN CHOW MEIN	107
CABBAGE ROLLS	108
CHINESE GREEN BEANS	109
AUTHENTIC CHINESE FRIED RICE	110
CHINESE STYLE KALE	112
CHINESE DOMPLINGS	113
CHINESE TEA EGGS (TAIWAN)	116
CHINESE BODDHA'S DELIGHT	117
Chinese proverb about money	118
CHINESE ALMOND COOKIES	119
OTHER CHINESE ALMOND COOKIES	120
CHINESE BROSSELS SPROOTS	122
MEAN CHINESE CHICKEN LO MEIN	124
CHINESE KONG PAO CHICKEN	126
CHINESE GINGER RICE	128
CHINESE LION'S HEAD SOOP	129
CHINESE SOOP SHAZAMI	130
CHINESE BAKED SWEET BREAD DOOGH	131
CHINESE CRISPY SPRING ROLLS	133
CHINESE NEW YEAR RICE	135
GAI LAN - CHINESE BROCCOLI - WITH OYSTER SAUCE	136
CHINESE BABY BOK CHOY	137
CHINESE FISH AND LETTOCE SOOP	138
CHINESE LONG NOODLES	139
CHINESE DRONKEN PRAWNS	141

STREET FOOD 143

POST SCRPTOM 145

Table of Contents 148

www.ingramcontent.com/pod-product-compliance
Lightning Source LLC
Chambersburg PA
CBHW041613220426
43670CB00001B/5